# CONTEMPORARY
# MINIATURE
# ROOM SETTINGS

# Contemporary Miniature Room Settings

Helen Ruthberg

Chilton Book Company · Radnor, Pennsylvania

Library of Congress Catalog Card No. 80-959
    ISBN 0-8019-6915-8 *hardcover*
    ISBN 0-8019-6916-6 *paperback*

Designed by William E. Lickfield

Manufactured in the United States of America

Photographs by Helen Karp Ruthberg
unless otherwise indicated

2 3 4 5 6 7 8 9 0    9 8 7 6 5 4 3 2 1

*In memory of my father,*
ELIAS,
*who appreciated*
*the United States of America*
*and freedom.*

# CONTENTS

# Preface

I WAS first introduced to miniatures as a young child. One of my girlhood friends owned a bookcase-style dollhouse which seemed awesomely perfect. I loved rainy days, because we played inside, and I had the opportunity to admire this "look but don't touch" dollhouse.

My next encounter with miniatures came when I was a college student. I never missed an opportunity to visit the display of tiny model rooms which all interior decoration majors were required to construct. Viewing these delightful miniature structures made from cardboard, fabric and scraps of everything was an enlightening experience.

Many years passed; during a family trip to the Smithsonian Institution in Washington, D.C., we came upon the marvelous Faith Bradford Dollhouse. I waved everyone on, explaining that I wanted to study this creation a bit longer. When everyone returned an hour and a half later, I was still glued to the spot.

When we returned home, I went underground. The basement became my retreat, where I threw myself into an ambitious program of creating miniatures. The more involved I became, the more I yearned to write about my interest. I wanted to share my joy with others.

Finally, in the early 1970s, interest in miniaturing began to blossom, and I decided it was time to begin writing. This book is about miniatures. I hope you like it.

# Acknowledgments

Compiling this book was a cooperative effort. The responses to my requests for assistance were both warm and gratifying. Special thanks go to the following craftspeople, who unselfishly shared not only their creations, but also instructions and patterns: Dee Snyder, Ann Maselli, Marilyn Davidson, Elaine Fleischman, Marilyn Diesu, and Kitty and John McKenna.

My gratitude is extended to Meg Nyberg, Anneruth Pfister, and Bede Pollets for their creative offerings. For special help, I thank Donna Murray and Sandi Doty.

Many others shared their creations and are credited where their work is shown.

I am grateful to Wendie Blanchard, editor of *The Miniature Magazine* and Carstens Publishing Company for permission to reprint my article, "Oriental World," originally published in *The Miniature Magazine*, Spring 1979.

I thank my husband, Jack. It takes great patience to live in our topsy-turvy house.

Finally, I would like to express my appreciation to miniaturists *everywhere*, whose personal expressions of enjoyment encouraged me to do another book.

# PART I

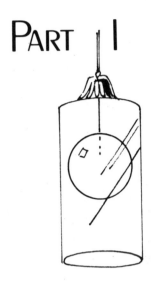

CREATING
CONTEMPORARY
MINIATURES

# 1

# Reproducing the Present

TODAY becomes yesterday. Yesterdays become yesteryear. And yesteryears become history, nostalgic and memorable.

We have all been exposed in one way or another to miniatures which, through the passing of time, have attained the status of "antiques." Whether these miniatures were hand crafted by artisans or made by less creative hands in a typical household, they have all earned respect and admiration. Except for occasional flights of fancy, most miniaturists have created accurate representations of households or room settings. We are fortunate to be able to view many of these dollhouses and rooms from the past in the sanctity of museums and private homes.

But today is crying out for its place in history too. Although collecting antiques and bits of nostalgia is very enjoyable, capturing and preserving a piece of the present can be even more fulfulling. Constructing miniatures with contemporary settings is an excellent way of representing today's life-style to future generations, and expressing your creativity at the same time.

Our everyday surroundings hold an abundance of ideas and themes ready to be incorporated into tiny replicas. Preferences for certain rooms are self-evident. Someone enjoys doing a kitchen; another person hates it. Nurseries may enchant some and bore others. And miniaturists are not limited to recreating home settings. Offices, shops, restaurants, theaters and other public places present rewarding challenges to many craftspeople. Your choice of room will depend entirely upon what you enjoy doing.

The biggest advantage of creating a room is that you are your own architect, builder, designer and decorator. Unlike moving into an apartment, house or condominium where the layout is already established, you decide where to place windows, doors, stairs and hallways.

Fig. 1–1 Portion of a living room, made by Jeanette and Martha Silver. A gift for their mother, the room reflects interests in her life and full-scale treasured objects. Family pictures are reduced photographs. The book jackets are cut from advertising and glued onto pieces of balsa wood. (Fred Mushel, photograph)

You select the finish for the walls, and you alone design and arrange all the details that make a contemporary miniature structure uniquely yours.

Expressions of contemporary design are not limited to home furnishings. Many stores, shops, offices, restaurants and entertainment areas have undergone face-lifts to reflect today's tastes and lifestyles.

Kitty and John McKenna blended old-fashioned architectural details with modern shop interiors in the fun but challenging project shown in Fig. 1–2 and Fig. 1–3. The exterior of the combined shops reflects the architecture of the past, but the interiors are contemporary.

New shops and entertainment areas that cater to present-day needs and desires provide miniaturists with many possibilities. Record shops, discotheques, and dollhouse and miniature shops are popular;

consignment shops are more stylish than the old second-hand stores; weight-reducing salons are much in evidence; quick-food establishments proliferate; and indoor malls are ever-growing.

One chapter cannot possibly cover everything about our time period, but the following information should increase your awareness and encourage you to express yourself more about the present-day scene.

## CONTEMPORARY DECOR

One dictionary defines contemporary as *"living, existing or occurring at the same time; of persons and things."* Of course, we are interested in things—objects that will be reproduced as miniatures.

Certain periods in history can be easily identified by specific dates. Georgian is dated from 1714 to 1795, more or less, and Victorian claims the years from 1840 to 1901, more or less. Our contemporary period will eventually be identified by a specific time slot, but for now, the catch-all phrases "modern" or "present-day living" best sum up our period.

Fig. 1–2 Kitty and John McKenna combined two shops in one "room." John milled the wood trim and made a standing seam copper roof. The jewelry display window has mirrors on the two rear walls. Colors are medium tan and white trim.

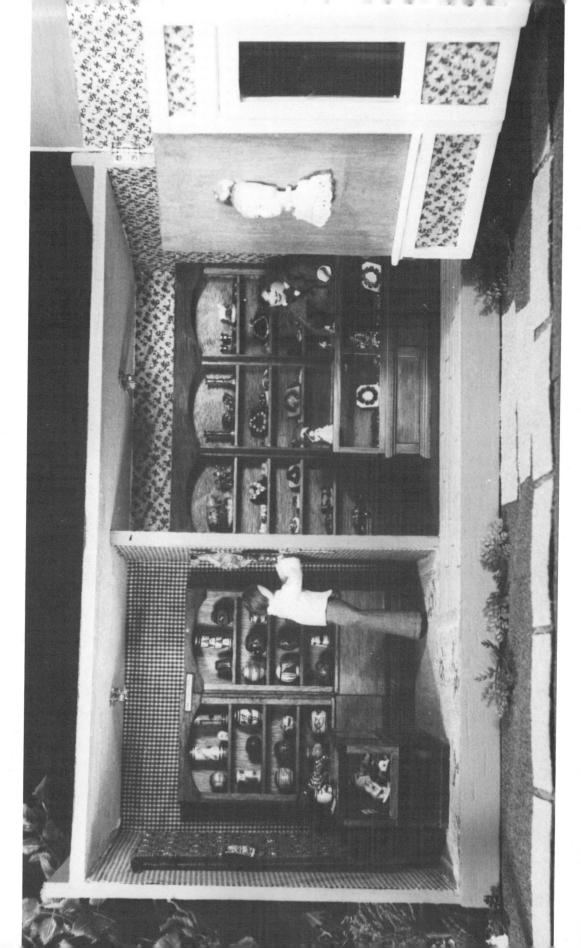

Fig. 1–4 Phyllis Katz decided that weight consciousness is very much a part of today. The reception room of a Diet Center is filled with advertising photographs, shelves of jars, books and bulletin board (left wall). The carpeting and dried flowers (right corner) are real, and the jars are packed with bits of real food.

The style of a period is expressed through interior decoration, the process of embellishing or making attractive the interiors of homes, offices, shops, buildings or whatever areas that make use of furnishings. A harmonious effect is created through proper selection of materials for walls, windows and floors; plus a pleasing color scheme, an interesting pattern and appropriate furniture and accessories.

Comfort, convenience and beauty are a part of today's decorating scheme. Layout and atmosphere are also important aspects in bringing the total effect together. Although style reflects whatever is currently fashionable, two schools of thought seem apparent in today's decors.

Fig. 1–3 The pottery shop is stocked with handmade beads resembling pottery. The "Temple Rug" on the left wall was made from the remains of an old beaded evening bag. A 50-year-old bracelet of carved ivory skulls and a soapstone monkey are among the merchandise. The fabric wall covering has one-quarter-inch brown checks. The jewelry shop has art objects and jewelry displays made from pieces of chain, rhinestones, beads and whatever. Sterling silver charms became statues. A calico print covers the walls.

Fig. 1–5 According to two enthusiastic miniaturists, our present scene isn't all Lucite and plastic. Jeanette and Martha Silver hark back to another day in their delightful vignette of Sally's Sweet Shoppe. The box is 14″ wide, 6″ deep and 9″ high. The following items were made: the box from ¼″ birch plywood; the frame from commercial molding; the Coca Cola crate and the shelves from balsa wood; the pretzels from self-hardening clay with sand used as salt; and the floor from black and white poster board cut into 1″ squares and glued down. The scene in the window is a postcard and the name on the top pane of "glass" was applied in reverse, using dry transfer letters. (Fred Mushel, photograph)

## Purist and Eclectic

Naturally there are purists in every era, requiring that all furniture, accessories, color schemes and construction details be authentically from one period. There is no mixing.

For contemporary purists, the emphasis is on "NOW." The decor is clean, lines are simple, color is clear and often vibrant, arrangements are informal and clutter is absent. The casual look predominates, and space-saving arrangements and contrasting textures are popular. Contemporary purists inspire and influence the use of today's materials, including exotic woods, Lucite, steel, aluminum, chrome, glass, polyurethane, fiberglass, vinyl and synthetic fabrics.

Eclectic decor is a combination of what seems best from two or more styles. Modern furnishings can look quite beautiful on an Oriental rug, and a Parsons table can mingle comfortably with traditional pieces. In eclectic contemporary design, the accent is definitely modern with peaceful coexistence between old and new, native and foreign.

Although casualness may still prevail, the mood is often transformed with opulent fabrics and accents of silver or gold. Eclectic remains in good taste through the years. Unbending to the latest fads or fashion, a mixture of different furniture styles provides warmth and lived-in appeal.

Although many eclectic room designs rely on a traditional decor, several other styles blend well in contemporary design. Oriental in contemporary decor highlights Eastern influence and bright colors. Provincial takes shape in country styles, while French pieces add a touch of formal elegance. Influenced by the Spanish, Mediterranean decorating uses heavy furniture and wrought iron designs. Mexican styles are rustic and warm. Colonial remains a classic, purposeful style, updated with bright, modern patterns and textured upholstery.

## Traditional

Traditional styling sits proudly side by side with contemporary, remaining a part of every era and every heritage. Each new period, however, adds its imprint upon existing period pieces. Contemporary

Fig. 1–6 A Contemporary sofa created by the author is structured from hardwood and upholstered in blue velvet. Simple and direct, it features two set-in pillows at each end, a popular contemporary designer scheme. Lucite stands, bottletop cube table and original water color are modern accessories.

influences may or may not be visible within the decorative scheme of the dedicated traditionalist.

## Ultramodern

Ultra means just that; it's the extra "push" using the latest, slickest, shiniest and most sophisticated furniture, accessories and decoration. Ultramodern design makes the most of today's metals and man-made products. An open, expansive look is achieved by using transparent furniture, and by decorating with glass, Lucite and mirrors. Art nouveau or art deco are sometimes incorporated in accent pieces. The overall effect is vibrating and stark.

## Revival

*Wicker* has made a big comeback, not only in reproductions of traditional patterns, but in newly designed furnishings.

The *baker's rack*, another old time favorite, has returned. Its airy, delicate structure fits into any room in the house or specialty shop. In addition to its original use, the baker's rack now turns up in living rooms as a plant stand, in dining rooms as a server, in bedrooms as a bookcase or useful holder, in bathrooms as a towel holder, in kitchens as a "whatever" holder and in restaurants as the dessert rack, of course.

*Bentwood* reproductions add a nice touch to the contemporary scene. Their sensuous curves soften the angular designs found in many modern rooms.

Fig. 1–7 Marilyn Davidson and Elaine Fleischman combine talents to produce their version of the ultramodern living room. They incorporate contrasting textures and see-through Lucite furnishings to create a chic yet comfortable room. Art deco designs—originals by Marilyn and Elaine—enhance the wall covering. You may know the artists better as "Minis by M.E." (Photo Illustration Center, photograph)

Fig. 1–8 A simulated wicker hanging chair and a baker's rack complement contemporary furniture. The author put this room together to show a blending of periods. The floor is vinyl tile and the walls are covered with blue and silver gift-wrapping paper. Perforated metal trim creates a partitioned room.

The revolving ceiling fan or paddle fan has found its niche in modern styling. Some fans team up with light fixtures, giving them a dual purpose.

Beautiful stained glass in windows, lamps and art objects adds a welcome touch to any room in a miniature display.

For the plump and cushy look, the *tuxedo sofa* has been updated and offers great seating comfort. The *Chesterfield sofa* is another old-time favorite beautifully clothed in solids or contemporary prints.

## Popular Furnishings

Some of the most popular pieces of furniture were designed years ago but continue to enjoy popularity. The Parsons table and the cube table are the most notable. They are simple to construct, but they cover a multitude of uses.

Originated at the Parsons School of Design in New York, the Parsons table is comfortable and at home with every decor. It has been covered with paint, paper and fabric, and has been constructed with metal, wicker and mirrors. It has been used as a coffee table, side table, console table, dining table, lamp table, bedside table, bench and desk. Its straight, classic leg design has been incorporated into chairs, sofas and bed frames.

The cube can't compete with the reputation of the Parsons table. Yet, what started out as a plain cube of wood has since been molded out of plastic and Lucite, and covered in a number of ways. As Fig. 1–9 shows, the cube is very versatile, particularly as a storage unit with or without a door.

Modular cabinet units are also distinctive contemporary furnishings, and modular upholstered pieces or sectionals are very popular.

Leather and vinyl upholstery combines with chrome and steel framework for modern chairs and sofas.

Lucite furnishings and glass tabletops create a clean, open atmosphere.

Molded plastic tables and chairs are popular and updated.

Platform furniture—beds, sofas, chairs—provides basic comfort and easy care.

### Accent Pieces

Baskets of any woven material find useful acceptance in many areas of a home or shop (see Chapter 8).

Pillows—an abundance of them—add a warm, casual touch. They can be solid colors, patterned, textured, crocheted, knitted, embroidered, needle pointed, batiked, appliqued. Line them up on a sofa, pile them up on a bed and stack some large ones on the floor.

Foreign art objects, especially from Mexico, Africa, the Orient or India, are very decorative.

Ceramic animals finished with white glaze or colored for a natural look have many uses. Small animals can decorate tabletops, while larger domestic animals can sit upon the floor.

*Hobby collections* of seashells, minerals, plates, etc., can be arranged and shown on a table, placed on shelves or mounted on a wall.

Macrame is most prominently used for plant hangings, but it can also be used to make wall decorations, handbags, and functional furnishings such as hammocks, swings, chairs, hanging tables, and swinging bassinets.

Weaving is very popular for creative wall decorations.

Plants can be hung from walls or set on floors, tables or specially crafted stands.

Fig. 1–9 The "cube" is a diversified unit often used as a table or as a storage unit for the floor or wall.

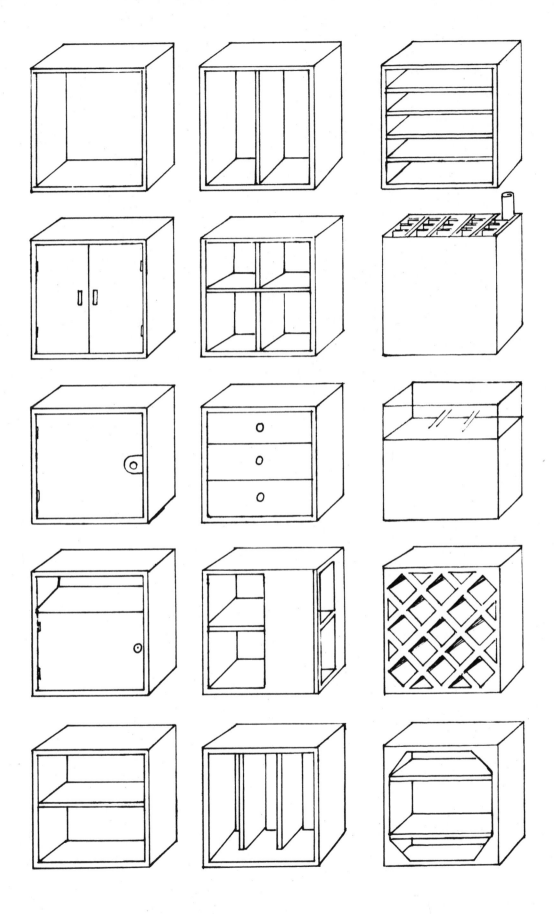

Fig. 1–10 Lucite is a popular choice for modern furnishings. With the exception of the lower left piece (a portion of a three-minute sand timer) all the plastic "tables" are actually display stands for gems: some are topped with glass.

## DESIGN AND CONSTRUCTION CONCEPTS
### Contemporary Room Planning

Many factors influence a room's layout, including its size, the window views, the structural design and the type of furnishings. The contemporary use of modulars, sectionals and platform furniture make interchangeable layouts possible.

Informal arrangements are popular in many modern room settings. Corner arrangements, pairs of love seats, clusters of comfortable small chairs and pull-up ottomans all contribute to more sociable seating layouts.

The center plan approach is also gaining appeal. Upholstered furnishings are brought into the room away from the walls, freeing wall areas for modular units or other essential furnishings. This arrangement depends upon the size of the room, but even small areas can utilize this concept, creating pit arrangements of L, U or C formations.

Contemporary bedrooms are also undergoing changes in layout. No longer just for sleeping, bedrooms have become living areas as well. A well-placed desk provides a quiet area for correspondence, and

Fig. 1–11 Pillows are neatly arranged along one side of a sofa-bed. They add a nice touch to an extra wide bed, usually adapted for apartment living (See Chapter 11). The painting is an original oil by the author. The petit-point rug is a finished kit from the collection of Catherine Callas Knowles.

a comfortable chair provides a peaceful retreat for reading and relaxation. The "island bed" concept is changing many conventional layouts, and the platform structure—centered in a room and partially surrounded by storage units, new walls and sectioned-off areas—creates a diversified arrangement.

## Color

The magic ingredient in most rooms is color. Bright or subdued, color can pull the furnishings and the different areas of the room together, and it can produce a powerful psychological effect as well. Color is expressed in many ways through paint, wallpaper, vinyls, fabrics, floor coverings and wood tones.

A color scheme is determined by various combinations of the six hues of the color wheel: yellow, green, blue, violet, red and orange (see Fig. 1–12).

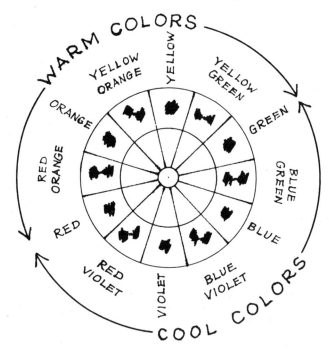

Fig. 1–12 The color wheel establishes color schemes and indicates warm and cool hues.

Complementary colors are exactly opposite each other on the color wheel: red and green; orange and blue; yellow and violet. Let's also include black and white, which are sometimes used for a most striking effect.

Analogous colors are next to each other on the color wheel: red, orange and yellow; yellow and green; green, blue-green and blue; green, blue and violet. Two, three or more colors can be included.

Triad is a combination of colors evenly spaced apart: yellow, red and blue; orange, green and violet. Sometimes a neutral color is used in place of one of the colors, such as in the popular scheme of red, white and blue.

A monochromatic scheme consists of one color. The value and intensity of the color can be altered by adding neutral colors to produce variations (maroon, red, pink).

*Value* is the degree of lightness or darkness of a color. Color values are called *tints* when mixed with white and *shades* when mixed with black.

*Intensity* refers to the brightness or dullness of a color, which is determined by adding gray.

Neutral colors are best used to pull many color schemes together. These include white, off white, ecru, gray, beige, tan and in rare instances, black.

Colors in their pure form are sometimes used. At their peak, colors do produce a striking effect, but most rooms look best with proper amounts of light and dark mixed with their colors.

Equal amounts of different pure form colors are rarely used within the same room, unless a wall is one color and another large area, such as carpeting, is another color. Usually, it is better to select a dominant hue and subordinate other colors to it. When in doubt, a good rule of thumb is: major, minor and small accents.

Choosing a color scheme for a particular room can be challenging but fun. The colors in a favorite fabric print could be the basis for a color scheme. A colorful rug or very special painting can also determine your direction. Understanding the color wheel will help you initiate your own scheme, but the easiest method is to browse through the pages of colorful books and magazines; you'll surely be smitten by more than one possibility.

### Light Fixtures

Lighting has arrived! Although they have long been used as technical necessities, lights are now an acceptable and decorative addition in contemporary decor.

Two forms of lighting illuminate a room: a general fixture for the entire area, and concentrated light for a specific spot. But the techniques for lighting are varied. Recessed spotlights in ceilings, cornice lighting and strip lighting for valances softly flood a room with controlled illumination. Panels of light also can be arranged on ceilings and walls.

Special lights can highlight a painting or mural, or spot a sculpture or other art object. A spotlight placed on the floor near a plant can create interesting effects. And if that's not enough, how about lights built into Plexiglas tables and other see-through furnishings? The miniaturist who is skilled in wiring can create some very unique lighting effects.

Lamps A, B, C, D and E in Fig. 1–13 are simulated pull down lamps. They are hung with either straight wire or coiled wire.

A. The top portion of a small, plastic asprin bottle serves as the shade. Cut the bottle along the dotted lines with a single-edge razor blade or sharp knife. Plug the upper hole with a round piece of wood, add a gold button (shank removed), a long-stemmed eyelet and hang it with florist's wire that's been painted and coiled around a thin stick. Use a bright bead for the light bulb.

B. The middle portion of the bottle is perforated with a needle to create a pierced design. Plug the upper opening with wood, and glue a plastic or metal button in the center. Drill a hole in the center of the button and wood, and fasten a wire through it. Add "light bulb."

C. The bottom portion of the bottle becomes the shade. Again, add a button or tall doo-dad, a long eyelet and coiled wire. Add "light bulb."

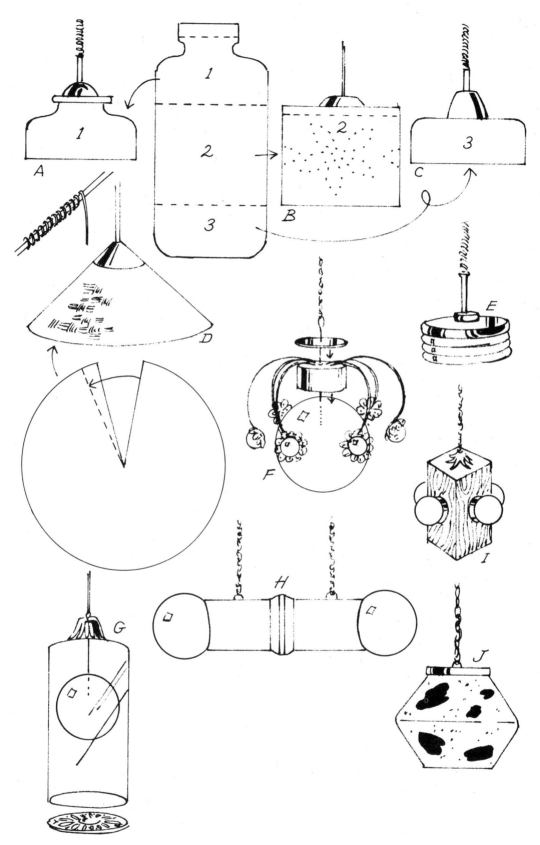

Fig. 1–13 Plans and suggestions for contemporary hanging light fixtures.

Paintings, carvings, ceramics, bric-a-brac and novelties are shown in a corner of Oriental World (Ch. 6).

One-inch-high metal collages can provide a theme for miniature rooms (Ch. 4).

Record albums, tapes and other accessories complete the Record Shop (Ch. 10).

A decoupaged console table and rattan table and chair are featured in the Garden Breakfast Room (Ch. 9).

Handmade baskets in assorted shapes are displayed in The Basket Stall (Ch. 8).

An Efficiency Apartment takes shape from an assortment of household throwaways (Ch. 11).

Ann Maselli's miniature workshop inside a shadowbox purse. (Ann Maselli, photograph)

A bird's-eye view of The Silver Greenhouse, constructed and furnished by Jeanette and Martha Silver. (Fred Mushel, photograph)

A formal dining room designed and built by Norman Forgue features an unusual window mural. (Larry De Vera, photograph)

A hand-painted mural of hanging planters is surrounded with embossed brick (Ch. 9).

(Above) Peter Westcott designed and created this spacious contemporary living room with a second-floor balcony and a patio at the rear. (Right) The patio outside Peter Westcott's contemporary house. (Neil Koppes, photographs)

A bi-level floor and shirred fabric background set off furnishings in the Contemporary Bedroom (Ch. 7).

Eclectic furnishings set off this Key West room, which has been designed and created by Dee Snyder. (Dee Snyder, photograph)

Miniature watercolors are matted and framed (Ch. 4).

D. Aida cloth or other stiff material is cut from the circular pattern shown. Overlap the sides of the V cutout to the dotted line and glue. Add a metal cone to the top and thread a wire through the center. Add "light bulb."

E. Glue three white plastic curtain rings together. On top of them, glue a lamp fixture check ring, a metal doo-dad and a long eyelet. Attach coiled wire and add "light bulb."

F. This globe fixture starts with a large roll-on deodorant ball. Make a hole in the top of the ball by forcing a heated pin into the center. A $1/4''$ ring of gold card is formed to be glued to the ball. Place cotton inside the ring and glue the gold circlet to the ball. Center the ring over the hole in the ball. Arc six cuttings of 18-gauge gold wire. Attach one end of each wire to a filigree and pearl (light bulb). When thoroughly dry, glue the other end of the wire to the cotton within the ring. Use a very tacky glue. Fit a $1''$ fastening pin through a flat metal disk or flat button. Push the pin through the cotton and into ball, adding gluing at each point of contact. Attach a fine chain to the top.

G. A fastening pin is pushed through a plain bell cap, the bottom of a clear plastic pill container and into a small roll-on deodorant ball. Add glue at contact points. An earring of flat filigree pearl is glued over the bottom opening, and a chain is attached to the top of the fastening pin.

H. A wooden macrame bead has two small roll-on deodorant balls glued at each end. Two chain links are opened and glued into drilled holes. Two chains are added.

I. Stain a $1'' \times 1/2'' \times 1/2''$ block of hardwood. Glue wide gold chain links ($5/16''$ diameter) to the center of each side, and glue white beads or

Fig. 1–14 The finished products for hanging lamps G, F, I and J in Fig. 1–13.

pearls over the links. Drill a hole through the center of the top of the wood. Flatten the prongs of a simple bead cap outward, and glue it to the top of the block with a fastening pin through it. Attach a chain to the fastening pin.

J. This shade is a beautiful ceramic macrame bead—white with bright spots of orange, red and black. The top opening is covered with gold card and a lamp fixture check ring. A chain is attached to the check ring, and a bead light bulb is added inside.

### Table Lamps and Floor Lamps

Shades for the lamps in Fig. 1–15 are made with the base of a small paper cup cut down to the desired size. The outer surface is covered with rice paper, calligraphy paper or a suitable material. Narrow strips of gold paper (greeting cards are good) or fine gold crochet thread can be added as trim to the top and bottom.

K. A ceramic table lamp that stands $3^{1}/_{4}''$ tall.

#### *Materials*

A $1^{1}/_{8}'' \times {}^{3}/_{4}'' \times {}^{3}/_{8}''$ block of balsa wood; 18 ceramic tiles ${}^{3}/_{8}''$ square (similar in color); ${}^{1}/_{8}''$ basswood strip (for corners); ${}^{1}/_{16}''$ brass square tubing (or equivalent); paper cup shade, covering for shade.

#### *Directions*

1. Drill a hole (view A) through center of balsa wood block to accommodate rod to be glued into place later.

2. Glue six tiles to the front and rear of wood block, and glue three tiles to each side (B view).

3. Cut gold card to fit over the top of the wood block and the tile edges. Pierce a hole in the card to match the hole drilled in the block, and glue it down.

4. Cut four strips of basswood $1^{1}/_{8}''$ long to fit the corners (view C). Paint the strips gold, and when dry, glue each corner piece into place.

5. Glue the rod into place.

6. Make shade and adhere to the top of the rod using gluey cotton for extra strength. Add an eyelet to the top as a finial.

L. Follow the same procedure as for K. Since this mirror table lamp is $2^{1}/_{4}''$ tall, the block of wood should be smaller. The mirror squares should be sized to fit the block of wood. Brass square tubing is used at the corners, and four clipped craft pins into the open tops of the corners.

M. A $3''$ antiseptic swab stick is glued to the bottom of a glass pill bottle. Use gluey cotton to hold the rod in the bottle, but be careful not to get glue on inner glass. When thoroughly dry, add miniature seashells, filling the entire bottle. Cap the bottle with a doo-dad, add two gold beads, a shade and a finial.

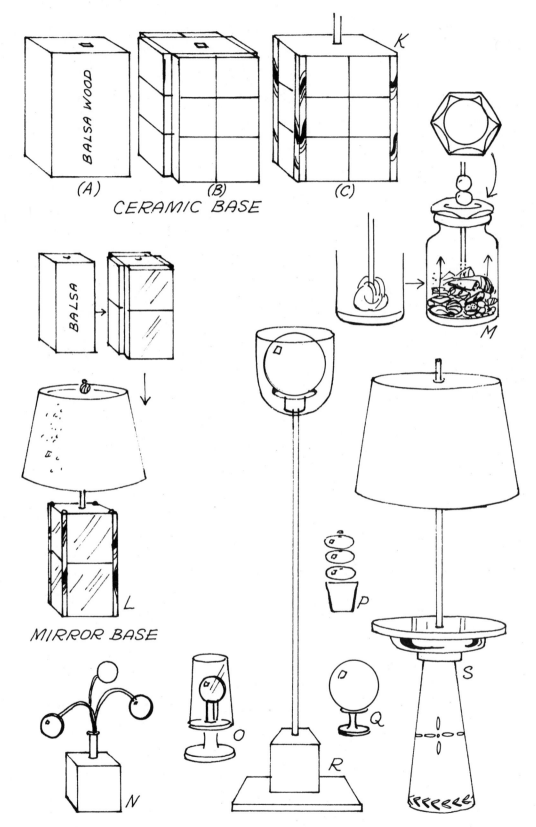

Fig. 1–15 Drawings and suggestions for table lamps and floor lamps.

Fig. 1–16 Hanging lamps A, C, D and E from Fig. 1–13, and table and floor lamps from Fig. 1–15.

N. A ½″ square macrame bead is the base. An eyelet, gold twisted wire and white beads complete the lamp.

O. A white plastic cuff link is the base, with a hole pierced in its top. An eyelet, pearl bead and a pin are glued together and into the hole. The see-through cover is from a spray bottle.

P. Three flattened beads are held together with a craft pin and glued to a small plastic bottletop.

Q. A large pearl bead is glued to a man's gold shirt stud.

R. The base is a rectangle of wood with a square macrame bead glued to it. Aluminum round tubing is glued into the bead hole. The plastic dome from a toy vending machine, a large wide eyelet and a small roll-on deodorant ball complete the top element.

S. A long wooden macrame bead is cut in half, painted black and decorated with gold paint. A lamp fixture check ring is glued to the

(Opposite page) Fig. 1–17 Suggestions for unique wall coverings.

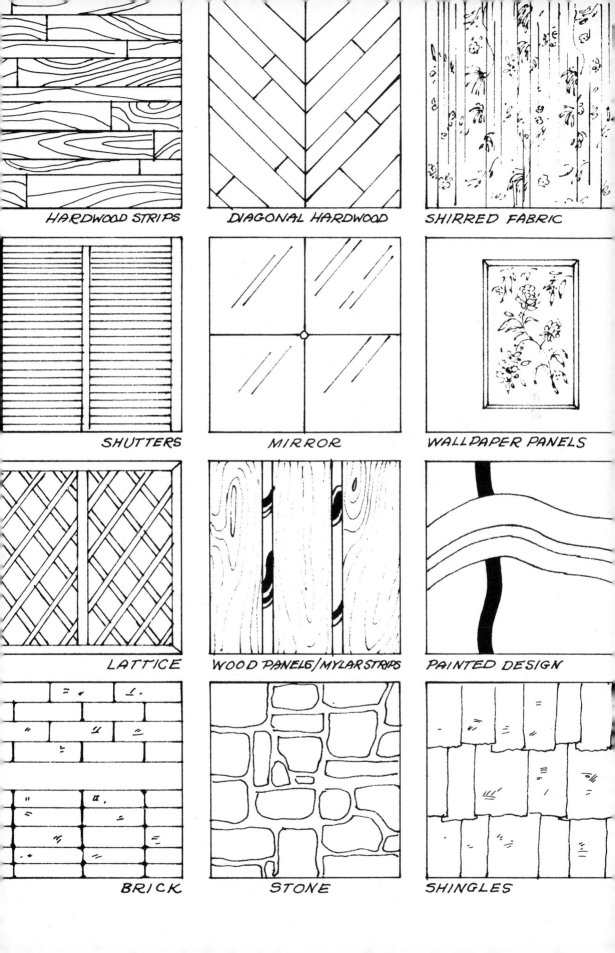

HARDWOOD STRIPS

DIAGONAL HARDWOOD

SHIRRED FABRIC

SHUTTERS

MIRROR

WALLPAPER PANELS

LATTICE

WOOD PANELS/MYLAR STRIPS

PAINTED DESIGN

BRICK

STONE

SHINGLES

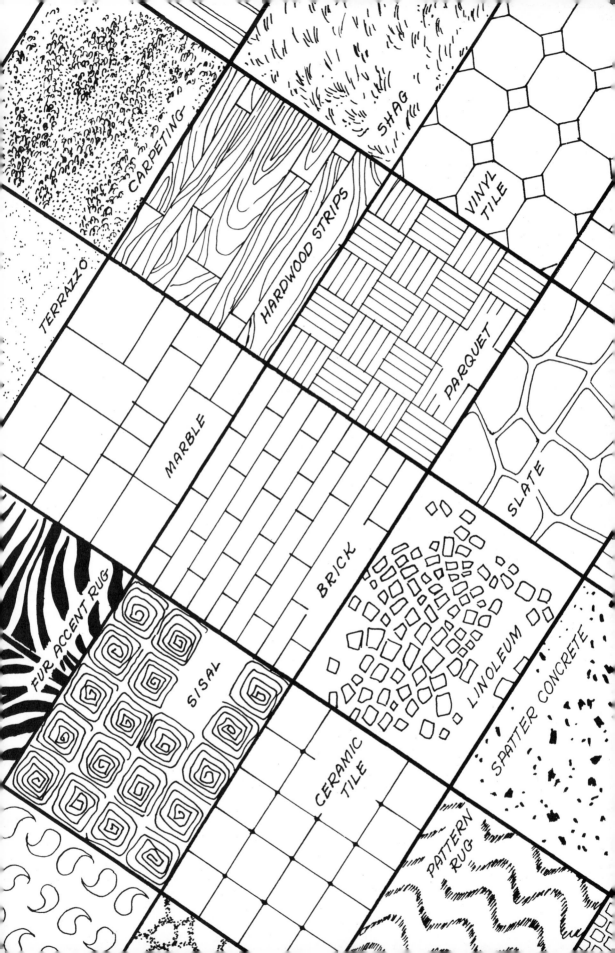

CARPETING

SHAG

VINYL TILE

TERRAZZO

HARDWOOD STRIPS

PARQUET

MARBLE

SLATE

FUR ACCENT RUG

BRICK

LINOLEUM

SPATTER CONCRETE

SISAL

CERAMIC TILE

PATTERN RUG

top of the bead, a 1¹/₂″ diameter wood circle (painted black and decorated gold) is glued over that. Drill a hole through the center to accommodate a rod, which is cut from a metal clothes hanger. Add the shade and finial.

## Contemporary Wall Coverings

Contemporary walls can be covered with paint, paper, vinyl, fabric or a number of unusual materials. Selecting the right wall covering will depend upon the atmosphere you want to create.

Painted walls remain unimportant if they are a background for several paintings and/or tall furnishings. Selecting the right color becomes the most important decision. Dark colors will make a room seem smaller and light colors will open it up. Walls can be shortened by bringing the ceiling color down onto the wall area.

Paper, vinyl and fabric wall coverings offer many patterns to choose from, including solids, stripes, vibrant plaids, luscious florals, super abstracts, terrific geometrics, imitative brick and wood, beautiful scenes and many more. Surfaces can be dull, smooth, slick, metallic, textured or flocked; and sometimes a combination of two or more finishes. Walls can be heightened by using a vertical pattern, or they can be widened by using a horizontal design.

Unusual materials means what it says. Wood panels in every conceivable finish are available for wall coverings. Decorators borrow from floor patterns, using parquet designs or various lengths of wood strips placed in horizontal or diagonal patterns. Panels can also be made from tiles, fiberglass, grass cloth, leather, latticework, carpeting and even Indian bedspreads. And don't overlook materials such as. brick, stone, shingles, mirrors, cork or barn siding.

## Floor Treatments

Floors can be rigid, resilient or carpeted.

Natural rigid flooring includes wood, brick, marble, slate, stone, terrazzo and ceramic tile. In fact, even concrete can make a stylish floor if finished properly.

Resilient floors are usually tiles made of vinyl, asbestos, asphalt, cork, rubber or inlaid linoleum. Their wide selection of designs and colors, plus their excellent simulation of hard floors, makes them extremely popular for almost any room.

Carpeted floors are being used more and more in restaurants and shops because they muffle noise. In the home, carpets and rugs provide a softness and warmth that blends well with all types of furnishings. Whether you choose an area or room-size rug, or wall-to-wall carpeting, the soft, textured floor covering is welcome underfoot.

*(Opposite page)* Fig. 1–18 Suggestions for different floor coverings.

SWINGING PANELS    ROMAN SHADE    SWAG & SHADE    ROLL-UP

TIE-BACK & SHADE    STAINED GLASS PANEL    SHUTTERS    VERTICAL BLINDS

POUF    LAMBREQUIN    DOUBLE TIE-BACK

Fig. 1–19 Window treatments are mostly simple and can vary with selection of materials.

Fur rugs are fluffy and luxurious. As a room-size rug or an accent piece, fur is totally sensuous.

A small, decorative rug placed on a solid-colored carpet will add a touch of interest to any room. This is where a tiny needlepoint or hooked rug is most welcome.

## Window Treatments

Windows deserve courteous attention and care. Besides being functional, they should be dressed in a fashionable way.

Fussiness is avoided in contemporary window treaments. Simple coverings are preferred, like drapes that tie back, glide on pull rods or are attached with rings. Sheer curtains and shades may or may not enhance a window. Fig. 1—19 offers many possibilities for window coverings.

# 2

# Tools and Supplies

SOME tools and supplies are essential, while others are designed to make the job easier. Working miniaturists accumulate tools and supplies according to their skills and endeavors. The more intricate and diversified their creations become, the more tools and supplies they require. Most miniaturists start out with the basics and gradually add to them as their skills and needs increase.

It is helpful to have most basic supplies readily available before starting a project.

## HOUSEHOLD SUPPLIES

Waxed paper to glue on (good because wax resists sticking)
Paper towels and rags (for painting on, for cleaning up)
Masking tape
Transparent tape
Pencils (medium-hard and hard)
Erasers
Scissors (regular and cuticle)
Tape measure
Metal-edged ruler
Cutting board (bread board, plastic board or even a smooth vinyl tile can be used)
Round toothpicks (for applying glue and making small structures)
Poultry skewer or large drapery hook (substitutes for awl; when heated, will pierce plastic)
Long, pointed tweezers for placing small items in position
Cotton balls and cotton batting (helps when gluing items together; acts as a filler)
Foam rubber

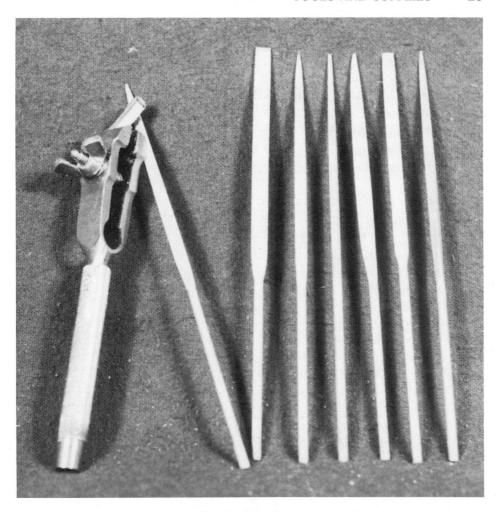

Fig. 2–1 A miniature hand vise will hold the tiniest of pieces for close trimming, sanding or shaping. An assortment of needle files help accomplish the job.

Permanent-color felt nibbed markers (Sharpie)
Emery boards
Clip clothespins and hair clips for clamping
Paper clips
Rubber bands
Applicator sticks, tongue depressors, popsicle sticks
Hairspray (stiffens fabric folds of curtains, drapery, tablecloths and garments)
Cleansing products (Lestoil for brushes, nail polish remover for fingers)
Empty deodorant jars with lids (to keep mixed paint from drying out; very handy storage containers)

Small juice cans
Cardboard
Straight pins

## STATIONERY, ART AND CRAFT ITEMS

Tracing paper
Sketching paper
Illustration board
3-ply Bristol board (useful for artwork, construction purposes and backing)
File cards (referred to as "card" in text)
Graph paper (helpful in aligning projects)
Drawing compass
Drawing pencils (HB, H and 2H)
Art foam (thin sheets of foam for upholstery use)
T square
Dividers
Stylus (small nib)
Brushes: rounds #000, #0, #3, others; brights #00, #2, others; aquarelle, #1 size
Triangles; 30°/60°/90° and 90°/45°/45°

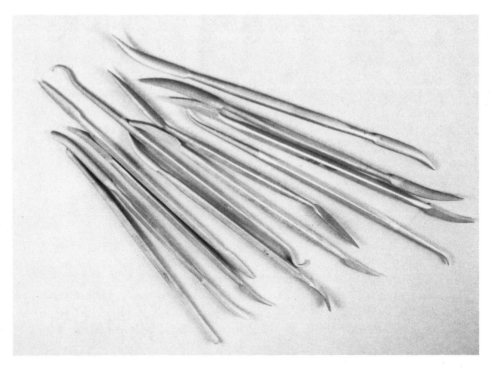

Fig. 2–2 Called *rifflers*, these unusual, handy files offer a varied assortment of tips, curves and hooks. Although they are considered luxury items rather than basic tools, they are most useful for getting into hard-to-reach places.

## CUTTING AND WORKSHOP TOOLS

Single-edged razor blades (several)
Pliers (needle nose, chain nose, serrated jaw)
Diagonal, semiflush wire cutter
Cutter for heavy wire
Set of needle files
Small hammer
Hand drill
X-ACTO knife and blades
X-ACTO miter box
Jeweler's saw
Fine-toothed razor saw
Soldering iron for liquid solder
Brads and small nails
Vacuum vise

## POWER TOOLS

Jigsaw (Dremel Moto-Shop)
Drill (Dremel Moto-Tool, variable speed)
Lathe (Dremel Moto-Lathe)

## ADHESIVES

The two adhesives most often used for bonding wood are yellow glue and white glue. Using either one requires a thin application to the two surfaces being joined together. Glue should be applied *after* the wood has been stained. Toothpicks are used for spreading glue onto small areas. Glues can be spread easily over a large surface with the edge of stiff cardboard.

Yellow glue is stronger and becomes tacky for quicker bonding. It does not dry clear.

White glue spreads easily and dries clear. It can also be used on paper, fabric and leather, and can be diluted with water.

Yellow glues—Titebond, Elmer's Carpenters, Willhold
White glues—Sobo, Elmer's Glue-All

A thick, tacky glue grips fast and works well on fabric surfaces. A very small item can be placed into position quickly.

Tacky glues—Velverette, Bond Instant Grip, Aleene's

Other useful adhesives are Epoxy glues, instant bonding glues (keep nail polish remover handy) and all-purpose glues.

## WOOD

Although Lucite and metals have made great inroads with contemporary furnishings, wood is still a popular material.

Balsa—soft wood, easily cut with a craft knife or single-edged razor blade; available in several sizes; sold in sheets and strips at hobby and craft stores; useful for furniture, accessory and interior construction

Spruce—medium-hard wood; sold in sheets and strips in better hobby and model shops

Basswood—medium-hard wood; sold in sheets and strips; available from dealers; this wood is usually used in commercial kits

Cherry, Walnut, Mahogany, Oak, Hard Pine, etc.—hardwoods of fine and coarse grain; require a power tool for cutting; available in blocks or sheets of limited sizes from advertized dealers or from local cabinetmakers

Dowels—hardwood with diameters of $3/32''$, $1/8''$, $3/16''$, $1/4''$, $3/8''$, $1/2''$, $3/4''$; very useful in miniature work; available in hardware, lumber and crafts stores

Plywood—available in thickness of $1/8''$, $1/4''$, etc., and in various woods; useful for wall construction

## FINISHING PRODUCTS

*Note:* Whenever sanding or applying a finish with a brush, always work in the direction of the wood grain.

Sandpapers—good quality *medium* for sanding box; *fine* and *very fine* for smoothing furniture surfaces

Steel wool #0000—for extra-fine finishing, surface is sanded with steel wool between coats of varnish

Tack cloth—specially treated cloth that removes lint and dust from wood surface prior to applying finishes

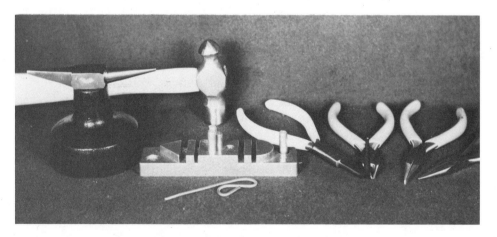

Fig. 2–3 A small anvil is used for hammering out warped metal, wire, etc. A wire bender (center) can produce a myriad of designs, limited only by the imagination of the miniaturist. An assortment of different pliers help to push and pull the wires.

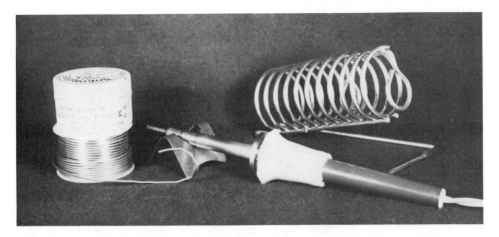

Fig. 2–4 Working with metals, a soldering iron may prove very useful.

Stains—there are water stains and oil-base stains. They come in a wide assortment of finishes, including birch, cherry, walnut, oak, mahogany and many others. Stain should be applied to light-colored woods (pine, basswood, balsa). One or two coats of stain are applied to wood *before* gluing pattern pieces together. Follow manufacturer's directions for drying time.

Sealer—shellac or varnish applied over stain

Fig. 2–5 Contemporary miniatures make much use of sheeting and round and square tubing made of brass, copper, aluminum and plastic. Sheets, rods, angles, tubing, bars and channel structures are available at model railroad hobby and miniature shops.

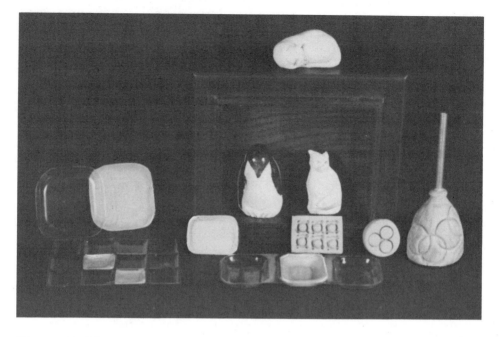

Fig. 2–6 Modeling compounds can be used to shape a variety of hard-to-find objects.

If a full-colored wood (cherry, walnut, mahogany, etc.) is being used, a clear (white) sealer is applied to the bare wood. In some products (i.e. Minwax, Sapolin and others), stain and sealer are *combined* in the same mixture.

Polyurethane varnish—glossy or satin finish

Wax—paste wax can be carefully buffed with a soft polishing cloth after 20 minutes; a second buffing is recommended for a smooth sheen

Acrylic spray—the fastest way to acquire a glossy surface; spray lightly or paint will run

Acrylic paints—for furniture; apply two coats and finish with a decoupage technique

Gesso—as an undercoat to seal wood before painting

## PINS

Straight sewing pins—from variety store
Round-headed pins—from variety store
Round map pins—from stationery store
Sequin pins (1/2″)—from crafts store
Brass escutcheon pins (5/8″)—from hardware store
Nail pins (1″, used for string art)—from crafts store
Fastening pins and head pins (used in jewelry work)
Hat pins
Push pins—from variety and art stores

Sometimes pins serve a useful purpose in pegging or fastening objects together, but more often they become a part of the decorating scheme. Selecting the right ones, they become drawer pulls; cabinet handles; simulated hinges on doors and cabinets; push buttons for this or that; numeral indicators on a clock; nailhead trim; bumpers for furniture legs; ping pong balls and golf balls (white, of course); covers for little bottles and tubes; knobs on television sets, radios, monitors; buttons on clothing and uniforms; and anything you can imagine.

## METAL SHAPES AND TUBING

Rods, tubing, angles and rectangles come in an assortment of sizes and metals including brass, copper and aluminum. Sheet metal and brass strips are also available. These products are usually sold in model railroad hobby shops. If no shop is convenient, order metals from a catalog (See Sources of Supply).

## ACETATE AND ACRYLIC

Acetate sheets are available at art stores and acrylic is purchased from crafts shops or glass dealers. Scraps of acrylic are sometimes left over from other cuttings. Some miniaturist dealers have thin sheets of acrylic available.

## MODELING COMPOUNDS

Modeling compounds are used to shape little items that may not be readily available. With them, you can sculpt food, dishes, bowls, animals, plants, flowers, lamp bases, dolls, toys, art objects or whatever else you may want to mold. In Fig. 2–7, shapes cut from clear plastic food trays make excellent molds for pressing a thin amount of modeling compound into depressed areas (left and center). When dry, these dishes, trays and platters can be painted and decorated. Sculptured animals are easily formed. Decorative wall plaques can be made by pressing interesting shapes into the compound (left). Lamp bases were modeled around aluminum rod and wired through tubing. Compounds used were Plastibo (air-drying), Plasmolegno, and an air-hardening wood compound which can be filed, sanded and sawed.

Different kinds of compounds are available. Some are rather firm and hard to knead; others are very soft and pliable. Some require baking, and others are air-dried. Available compounds are Sculpey, Super Sculpey, Fimo, Plasmolegno, Plastibo and Repla-Cotta. Ask other miniaturists how they like a particular product.

Of course, you can always whip up a batch of bread dough, described in *The Book of Miniatures: Furniture and Accessories* (Chilton Book Company).

# 3

# COMBINING MINIATURES WITH Useful Items

THE first Boca Raton Miniature Show I participated in introduced me to an entirely new concept in miniatures—decorating useful objects with miniature displays. As miniaturists approached my table, I saw *shadow-box purses*, handbags with miniature scenes built into one side of the carrying cases.

After admiring an enchanting lamp base complete with a miniature scene, I began thinking about other ways that miniatures could be combined with useful objects. The following suggestions are intended to spur your imagination and to demonstrate how useful contemporary miniatures can be.

## SHADOW-BOX PURSES

Shadow-box purses, commonly called box purses, have been decorated in different ways for years. Everything from three-dimensional paper tole to dried flower displays has adorned these functional showcases. Now miniaturing has entered the scene.

The depth of the shadow box in Fig. 3–1 is a mere $2\frac{1}{4}''$, but Ann Maselli's imagination has filled those few inches with a delightful scene. A multi-talented miniaturist who also teaches the craft, Ann has created a "Miniaturist's Work Shop" scene within her box purse. All the necessities for miniature crafting are reproduced in their tiniest form. All the items on the workbench, the remarkable miniature dollhouse, and most of the furnishings are handmade. Ann's directions for making the box and the miniature dollhouse follow.

Fig. 3–1 Ann Maselli's rendition of a box purse, complete with a miniature workshop scene. The furnishings (except the chair and books) are handmade, the painting is her original and the sitting doll is sculptured. All items on the basswood workbench are handmade, as is the dollhouse. (Ann Maselli, photograph)

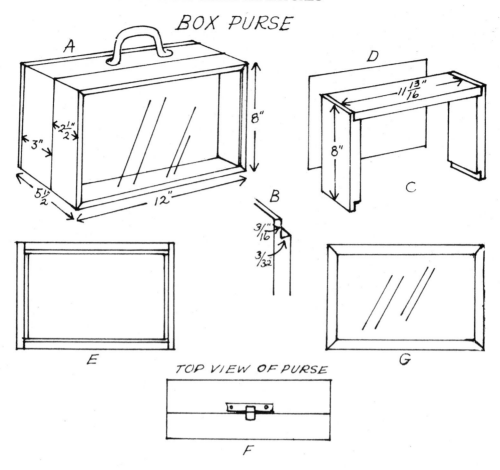

Fig. 3–2 Direction drawings for box purse.

## MAKING A BOX PURSE

by ANN MASELLI

The purse is made of *two separate boxes,* and its overall dimensions are 12″ long, 8″ high, 5½″ wide (see view A). The purse part of the box measures 12″ long, 8″ high and 3″ wide. Using basswood 3″ wide and ³⁄₁₆″ thick, cut two pieces 11¹³⁄₁₆″ long and two pieces 8″ long. Groove each end of the 8″ pieces as shown in view B. The grooved ends help support the top and bottom pieces (see view C). To make the back D, use ⅛″ plywood (available at hobby shops) cut to fit the outside edges. Use very thin brads and glue on all joints. If the purse is to be stained, do so before gluing.

The front section is constructed in the same manner, but is 2½″ wide. The plywood back is cut to fit *inside* the shadow box, and is

(Opposite page) Fig. 3–3 Patterns and instructions for miniature dollhouse.

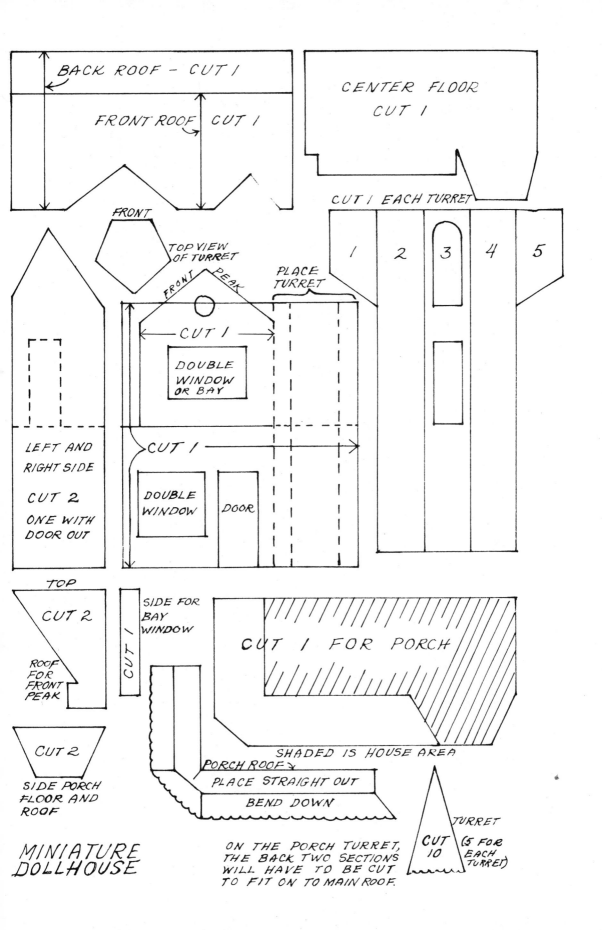

BACK ROOF - CUT 1

FRONT ROOF CUT 1

CENTER FLOOR CUT 1

FRONT

TOP VIEW OF TURRET

CUT 1 EACH TURRET

1   2   3   4   5

FRONT PEAK

PLACE TURRET

CUT 1

DOUBLE WINDOW OR BAY

LEFT AND RIGHT SIDE

CUT 2

ONE WITH DOOR OUT

CUT 1

DOUBLE WINDOW

DOOR

TOP

CUT 2

ROOF FOR FRONT PEAK

CUT 1

SIDE FOR BAY WINDOW

CUT 1 FOR PORCH

CUT 2

SIDE PORCH FLOOR AND ROOF

PORCH ROOF

PLACE STRAIGHT OUT

BEND DOWN

SHADED IS HOUSE AREA

MINIATURE DOLLHOUSE

ON THE PORCH TURRET, THE BACK TWO SECTIONS WILL HAVE TO BE CUT TO FIT ON TO MAIN ROOF.

TURRET

CUT 10 (5 FOR EACH TURRET)

Fig. 3–4 A close-up view of the miniature dollhouse created by Ann Maselli. Use this photo as a guide for placing pattern pieces into proper position. (Ann Maselli, photograph)

Fig. 3–5 A metal bookend and an Heirloom craft box are destined for a bookend miniature project.

glued in place. Glue ⅛" square strips to the outside edges of the shadow box (see view E) to make a frame for the Plexiglas front.

The inside of the purse and the rear wall of the shadow box are covered with a quilted material. Attach the two boxes with hinges on the bottom and a centered clasp on the top. While fastening them together, hold them in place with tape.

The handle is carved wood; the word "miniature" and the leaf decorations are burnt in with a wood-burning tip on a soldering iron. Center the handle on the back section, but as close to the joint as possible (see view F).

If you did not stain your box, now is the time to paint it.

After you have decorated the display area, cut a piece of Plexiglas to fit inside the frame made with the ⅛" square wood strips. Hold the Plexiglas in place with a frame made from 1/16" × ⅜" strips of wood. Miter the corners (see view G). Tape the frame and Plexiglas in place; drill very small holes in the edges of the frame and use No. OX ⅜" screws (available at Train or Hobby Shops) to screw on the frame.

Add four feet to the bottom of purse.

Fig. 3–6 The Heirloom box is converted to a bookend and a miniature display. Small plant arrangements were made by Audrey Diener.

## A MINIATURE DOLLHOUSE

by ANN MASELLI

The dollhouse is made from ⅛″ thick wood, which is purchased already scribed to look like siding. Cover the back of all wood with masking tape when scribing to keep it from splitting.

Fig. 3–7 "Country Kitchen" lamp by Bob Wittman. (Baleno Studio, photograph)

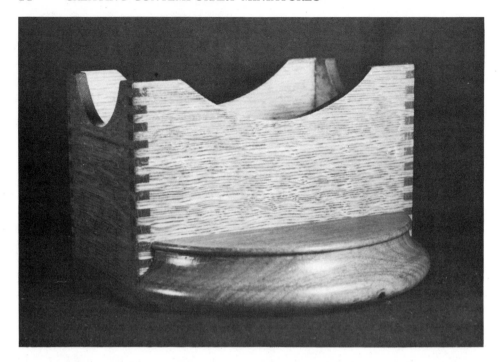

Fig. 3–8 An old oak file box and part of a round tray (turned upside down) combine to become useful miniatures in different ways.

Railings, doors and windows are HO gauge model railroad size. Inside of house is incomplete; cut windows and doors as needed. Cut all roofs from cardboard and use HO roofing to cover them.

Assemble the house by following the directions on the pattern pieces in Fig. 3–3, and by observing the photograph of the dollhouse (Fig. 3–4).

## BOOKENDS

The bookend display shown in Fig. 3–6 resulted from the purchase of a pair of small Heirloom boxes. Their width happens to conveniently match the width of metal bookends. The Heirloom boxes were painted and finished with Hermes roof paper and a dark brown cotton print fabric on the inside. A generous assortment of molded plants, flowers and containers, and a macrame hanging, all made by Audrey Diener, decorate the inside. The front can be covered with Plexiglas for protection.

## LAMP BASE

The base of a lamp provides an ideal stage for a miniature scene. The basic structure of the lamp can be purchased, and you have an almost unlimited number of styles and sizes to choose from. The

Fig. 3–9 A brightly colored plastic flower arrangement within the file box is complemented by a miniature flower arrangement and porcelain vases.

contemporary miniature scene can reflect the theme of the room in which the lamp is used, such as a child's room or a den, or it can be designed as part of the room's decor.

Handmade lamps are a specialty of miniaturist Bob Wittman. The lamp in Fig. 3–7 has a "Country Kitchen" scene in its basswood base, complete with a handmade rocking chair, cast-iron stove, wooden refrigerator and cornhusk doll. The base measures 15½″ × 8½″ × 9½″, and the lamp is 30″ tall. Bob enclosed the miniature scene with acetate to protect it.

Fig. 3–10 The file box becomes a napkin holder. Filled and corked glass bottles, and sterling and copper pieces are arranged as a handsome miniature display. The box could also become a letter holder.

## FILE BOX

Sometimes odds and ends can be put together to create a useful item with a contemporary miniature setting. An old wooden file box and a round wooden tray cut in half and turned upside down combine to make several useful miniatures. Figures 3–9, 3–10 and 3–11 demonstrate some of the possibilities. Besides being used as the obvious file for recipes, the file box can also become a letter holder, napkin holder, plant holder and dried flower holder.

## PENCIL HOLDER

Pencil holders come in an assortment of sizes, shapes, designs and finishes. Attaching one to the side of a boxed miniature vignette adds a new dimension to this useful commodity. Some holders are square but

Fig. 3–11 A planter and variegated philodendron are placed within the file box, and Chinese miniatures rest on the platform.

most are round, requiring some creative construction to attach them to boxes.

The useful miniature in Fig. 3–12 began with the purchase of a box with a scalloped opening. I selected Hermes wallpaper with a heart pattern and used a valentine handkerchief for the dressing table. The predominantly red and white colors are set off by gold trim on the mirror frame and toiletry articles made from assorted baubles. A piece of acrylic covers the front, held in place by four screws which are hidden beneath four beautiful filligree bell caps. The wooden pencil holder is securely glued in place.

## CLOCK

What could be more useful than a clock? And what could be more attractive than having a miniature display nestled above or below the faceplate of a time piece? Crafts shops sell boxes which are purposely made for clock fanciers. Battery-operated, they can be transformed into combination clock-miniature displays.

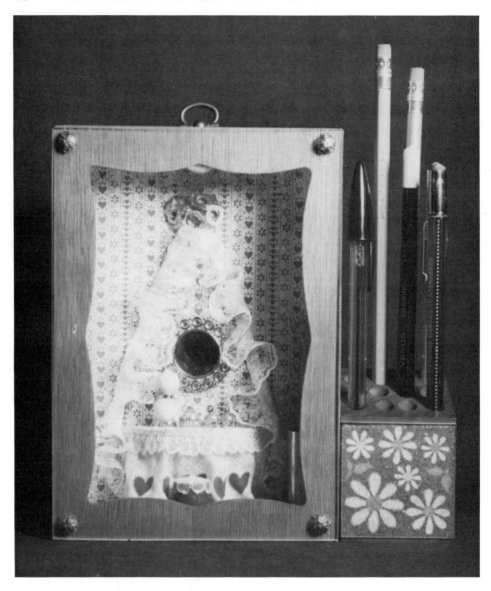

Fig. 3–12 A pencil holder is attached to a miniature display with a valentine motif featuring a dressing table.

Some box clocks come with additional cubby-holes that can be used for a miniature display, but most are single units for clocks only. But with a little carpentry work, an astute builder can construct a distinctive creation. Techniques for finishing off the box include painting, staining, decoupaging, tole painting, bread-dough designs, fabric covering or ribbons and trim.

# 4

# Art, Handicrafts and Frames

CONTEMPORARY paintings can run the gamut from simplicity to intricate detail. Modern designs often are painted in colors of vibrant intensity. Line drawings can be brightened with color washes, and portraits can be simple in technique and rendering. Nature is a favorite subject matter among contemporary artists and designers, so use butterflies, flowers, plants, trees, seashells, insects, and animals for a pleasant blending of furnishings and wall decor. Free-form spatter designs and abstracts can change the whole "tone" of a room. These can be placid, wild, aesthetic or explosive, depending upon your own personal approach.

Wall murals must be carefully thought out, because mistaken dimensions or poor color selection can cause untold grief. Murals are painted before the wall structure is nailed together, or a mural can be painted onto good quality art board cut to the wall size. Try to place the major furnishings in front of the wall before final assembly. It is heart-breaking to have to disassemble a room, if you find the wall does not "fit in."

Geometric designs can also be applied directly to the wall. These can be put on with paint, or they can be applied with cut-outs of colored tape fastened to the wall with their own sticky backing.

A family tree mural could be quite charming in the proper setting. Prepare a tree design; paint it onto the wall, and hang tiny framed pictures of family members on the branches.

## WATERCOLOR PAINTINGS

I call these "watercolor whimsies." They have a light and airy feeling and they're really very easy to do. It takes practice and a little trial and error, but the fun involved is a bonus.

49

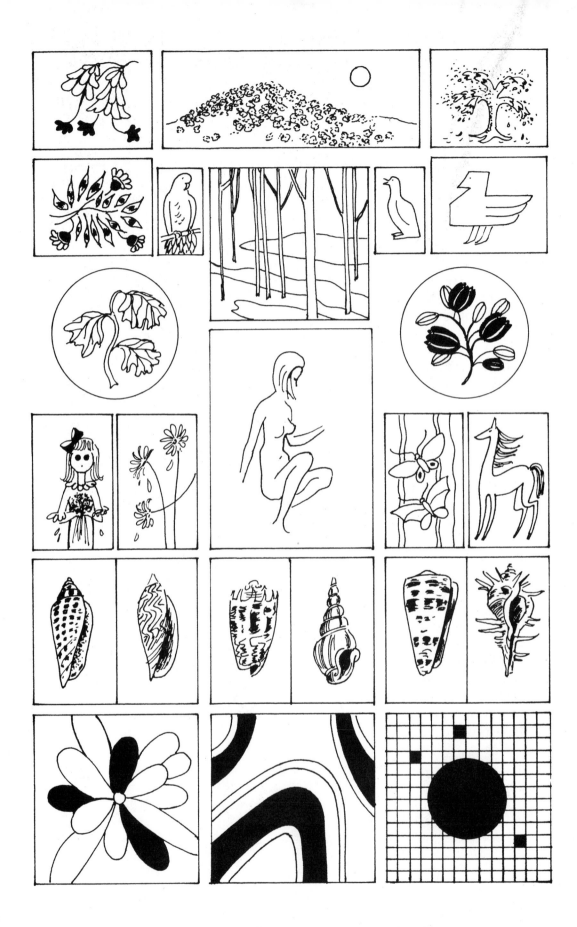

The unusual finished effect of "whimsies" results from particles of table salt sprinkled onto the wet colored surface of the painting. The salt gives the paintings a "fairyland" effect.

### Materials

Heavy watercolor paper (smooth surface) from art supply store cut to 3″ × 4″, 2″ × 3″ or size you prefer; watercolor paints (Windsor Newton or Grumbacher); water color brushes: rounds #00, #3; brights #7; paper toweling and paper tissues; table salt.

## Directions

Plan some little sketches on paper.

The entire surface of paper is thoroughly moistened with clear water, but not soaked.

Sky is applied with blue-colored tint. Another color can be brushed into the blue. A swish of gray color will make the sky look stormy. A touch of orange or vermillion at the right spot will suggest a sunset.

Now quickly add something in middle section: green grass, brown rocks, tan sand, mountains, small forest of trees or whatever you think you want. Single simple strokes are all that you use. This must all be done quickly before the wet surface begins to dry. Try to always leave some small areas of white paper showing and if it's a snow scene, *lots* of white paper showing. While still moist, lightly sprinkle salt onto selected areas. Don't use too much salt and *don't* sprinkle over the *entire* painting. Allow to dry completely.

When dry, shake off loose salt. Painting is now ready to receive any tiny detail painting that you may want to add to make the scene more interesting. Minute people, trees, houses, rocks, stumps, animals or grass stalks are added to foreground, *only* if you think your painting needs this extra touch.

Fig. 4–2 shows some of the results; two and three colors are often sufficient to achieve the desired mood.

Your finished painting can be bordered with a white or colored mat, covered with thin acetate or acrylic and framed in a simple manner.

## MACRAME

The abundance of talent in the world is never ending and when it's translated into miniature, the effect is awesome. Marilyn Diesu is a multi-talented artist and craftsman. When Marilyn consented to design

Fig. 4–1 Selection of wall art depends upon preferences. This assortment shows some of the many designs that can be used.

Fig. 4–2 Watercolor Whimsies made with wet-in-wet technique. Background edges are softly blurred and faintly discernible.

Fig. 4–3 Marilyn Diesu made a white hanging table (6½″ long), dark blue wall hanging (5½″ long), white pillow, and miniature weaving to help decorate the author's rooms.

and make a miniature macrame hanging table, I was totally unprepared for her exceptional finished masterpiece. Intricately knotted with crochet thread, it features two levels for plants or art objects. Macrame enthusiasts will delight in making this lovely creation.

And then while Marilyn was still in the spirit of miniature making, she also created a macrame wall hanging. It's an elegant piece and will enhance any miniature room. I used it in my Contemporary Bedroom (chapter 7). Marilyn also made a tiny macrame pillow, and for good measure, added a charming bit of weaving.

For those who are trying macrame for the first time, Fig. 4–4, 4–5 and 4–6 show the basic knots needed for these projects.

## HANGING TABLE

by MARILYN DIESU

### *Materials*

3 rings $3/8''$, $5/8''$, $3/4''$, two acrylic rounds $1''$, $13/4''$ diameter, DMC #5 Perle Cotton. (Round mirrors can be substituted for acrylic.)

### *Directions*

Cut 16 cords, 1 yard each.

Cut and set aside for later use: 16 cords $3/4$ yard each; 8 cords $1/4$ yard each.

Put 1-yard cords through smallest ring so that the cords hanging down on one side are 10 inches long and the other ends are 26 inches.

Holding all cords together, set two long cords to the left and two long cords to the right of all other cords and do about ten half-knots.

Spread out on macrame board and divide into groups of four cords each, alternating one group of long cords and one group of short cords.

Do a sinnet of five square knots on each group.

Double-half-hitch all cords to second (middle size) ring. Keep groups of short cords alternating with groups of long cords.

Work a sinnet of two square knots with each group of four cords. Alternate and repeat. Alternate and repeat again.

Double-half-hitch all cords to third (largest) ring, making sure to keep groups of cords together, one short group of four, one long group of four, etc.

Work three square knots on each group of short cords. Hold all short cords together in center under ring and make a wrap around all short cords.

Cut a tassel to $3/8''$.

With long cords make half-knots sinnets $31/4''$ long, and set aside for now.

Fold the $3/4$-yard cords in half one at a time and larkshead two cords on each side of short cords. You now have four cords hanging from each side of short cords. With each of these groups of four cords, do nine square knots.

Twist the fourth cord from group on left of short cords around first cord of next group (group on opposite side of short cords), make 15 more square knots on each sinnet. Measure down $1/16''$ and do one alternating square knot row. Measure down $1/4''$ and tie a wrap. Cut cords to $5/8''$ tassel.

Pick up group of long half-knot sinnets. Divide the four cords into two groups of two cords each. Fold one $1/4$-yard cord in half and lay

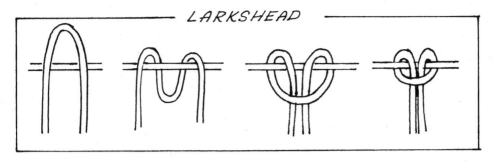

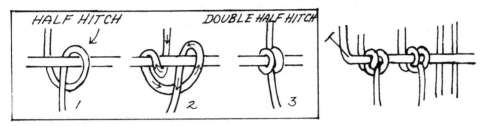

Fig. 4—4 These diagrams show tying of larkshead, half-hitch, and double-half-hitch. Drawing on right is a horizontal row of double-half-hitches, using the first cord as the holding cord.

Fig. 4—5 Tying a wrap-knot.

Hold all cords together except two.

Place one of those two in an "S" shape and hold it together with the other cords, keeping the top loop of the "S" higher then the top of the finished tassel.

Take the other free cord and wrap it from the bottom of the section you want to wrap. Wrap around all the cords including the "S" shaped one (view #2). Continue wrapping all the way up to the top, fairly tightly.

Take the end of the "wrapping" cord and put it through the top loop of the "S" (view #3).

Now take the bottom loop of the "S" at point "B" and the end, point "C" and pull down, while holding the wrapped section so it won't slip (view #4). Pull down until the top loop comes through, bringing the wrapping cord end with it. Now pull the wrapping cord until it comes all the way through causing the whole knot to stay secure. The wrapping cord will be shorter than the rest.

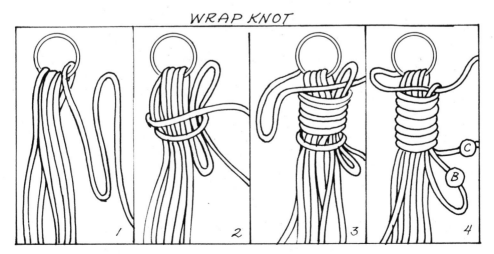

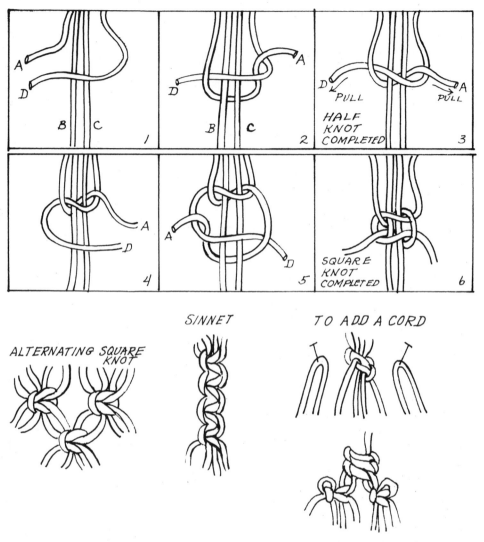

Fig. 4–6 Tying a half-knot and square knot.

Four cords are used to tie a square knot.

First arrange cords so that the two center cords B and C hang down close together and cord A is out of the way. With cord D arrange so that you have the *look* of the letter P (view #1). Now, cord A goes over the horizontal part of cord D and under cords B and C and from underneath, up and out through the loop of the P (view #2).

Now pull cords A and D so they are taut (#3).

You have completed a half-knot at this point. When repeated several times, the knot will twist by itself.

To complete the square knot repeat the same steps in reverse.

First make the letter P reversed. Cord D (that now hangs on the opposite side of the knot) goes over cords B and C. Then A goes over the horizontal part of D and under B and C and from underneath up and out through the loop of the P (#5). Pull cords A and D tightly to finish (#6).

To add a cord from a sinnet (a downward row of knots) of four cords, fold two cords in half and pin one to each side—you will then have eight cords, with which to do two square knots.

folded end next to one group of two cords and do one square knot. Repeat with other two-cord group.

Work one alternating square knot with the four inner cords.

Repeat with the three sinnets of half hitches.

About 1/4″ down work one row of alternating square knot cords, two adjacent ones from each group.

About 1/4″ down put all cords from all four groups together and tie a wrap. Cut tassel the desired length.

## WALL HANGING

by MARILYN DIESU

### Materials

#3 DMC Perle Cotton; 1/8″ dowel or branch 1 1/2″ long.
Macrame board and T pins. Finished length hanging 1″ by 5 1/2″.

### Directions

Cut ten cords 1-yard long (cords do not have to be that long, but it is easier to knot if at least that long).

Larkshead all cords to dowel.

Knot two rows of square knots (five square knots across row).

3rd row—alternating row. Leave out two cords, tie four square knots across row, leave out two cords on end.

4th row—leave out four cords, tie three square knots, leave out four cords on end.

5th row—tie two square knots leaving out six cords on each end.

6th row—tie only one knot in center (leaving eight cords out on each end).

7th row—leave out six cords, tie two square knots and leave six cords out on end.

8th row—leave out four cords, tie three square knots, leave out four cords on end.

9th row—leave out two cords, tie four square knots, leave out two cords on end.

Now tie five sinnets (using all cords), each one five square knots long.

Using first cord on left as holding cord, tie a row of double-half-hitches using all cords. The holding cord will now hang down on the right side of all cords.

Tie five half-knot sinnets of about seven half-knots each across row.

Tie a row of double-half-hitches from right to left using the first cord on right (this is actually the same cord going back) as the holding cord.

Tie a row of five square knots using all cords.

Repeat rows 3 through 6.

Using the first cord on left as holding cord over the next nine cords, right below square knots, tie a diagonal row of double-half-hitches. Repeat the same procedure from the right—using the first cord from the right. With the two center cords (the cords that were holding cords) double-half-hitch one over the other. With the four cords on the left tie a sinnet of four square knots. Repeat with the first four cords on the right.

With the next four cords from each end tie two more sinnets of three square knots.

With the four center cords, tie one square knot. Repeat rows 3 through 6 again.

Repeat the diagonal double-half-hitches again.

With the first six cords on left, tie a wrap $3/8''$ down; repeat on right.

With eight cords in center, tie a wrap $1/2''$ down. Cut cords to desired length leaving the center group longer.

## PILLOW

> by MARILYN DIESU

### *Materials*

Three yards of 3-strand persian needlepoint yarn, scrap of fabric and stuffing for pillow, macrame board and T pins, masking tape, crochet hook.

### *Directions*

Cut seven lengths of yarn 15″ each. Separate each of the three strands into individual strands and lay 20 strands side by side on macrame board. Tape top edge to board with masking tape.

About 4″ down, tie a row of five square knots across using four strands for each square knot. It should measure about 1″ across.

Alternate and tie a row of four square knots, leaving two strands out at each end. Repeat these two rows until you have 13 rows. It should measure about an inch long.

This completes the knotting to make a 1″ square pillow with fringe on top and bottom. Cut fringe. Fold a scrap of this yarn in half and larkshead into a space on the side that was created by the alternating row of square knot. This can be done more easily with a crochet hook. Fill in as many down the sides as necessary for the fringe to be as full as the other two sides. Trim all fringe approximately $3/8''$.

Make a 1″ square pillow from desired fabric and blind stitch the macrame square around the edges of the pillow.

## LATCH-HOOK RUGS

Meg Nyberg specializes in miniature latch-hook rugs and her lovely creations show her enthusiasm for this craft. Responding to my request, she designed the contemporary rug that is pictured in Fig. 4–7

Fig. 4–7 The latch-hook rug or wall hanging was designed and hooked by Meg Nyberg who specializes in this craft. Finished size is 3¼″ × 2¼″.

and in the contempory bedroom. The color scheme is low-key, with white, black and gray for the house. A cream-colored path advances toward the door. Pink and rose flowers in window boxes and in the foreground mingle with green leaves and grass. Sections of the floral and leaf display were worked with a higher pile, giving an added dimension to an already beautiful wall hanging.

The materials that Meg uses are a very tightly woven muslin, one strand of DMC six-strand embroidery cotton and the "Boye Rush 'n Punch" punch needle, which is adjustable to two different hooking heights.

## BATIK

Batik is a craft which uses wax-resist dyeing to create designs or pictures on natural fabric of cotton, silk or linen. The finished batik can be framed, or used anywhere you would normally use material—curtains, upholstery, tablecloths, pillows, or doll's clothing.

My friend Bede Pollets, who has had experience with batik, answered an SOS and obligingly rendered some petite miniature designs, all in a free-form style. For instructions on how to do batik, visit your local library and borrow a book on the subject or get a copy of *The ABCs of Batik* (published by Chilton Book Company).

Fig. 4–8 These batik free-form designs are the creation of Bede Pollets. A fascinating craft, batik can enliven a wall as a beautiful and unusual accessory.

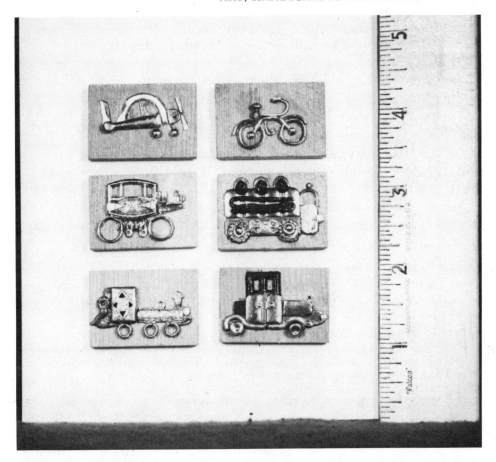

Fig. 4–9 An assortment of metal scrap, jewelry findings, odd bits of plastic, and tiny jewels for lights produced these enchanting transportation collages.

## COLLAGES

Certain miniature items seem to cause an undue flutter of ooh's and ahh's; miniature collages often cause this reaction. There's something quite appealing about all those unaccountable little items fitted together to create an artistic arrangement. Collages can be made from several types of material.

### Metal Collage

One of my favorite types of collage makes fascinating usage of everyday items to create cars, trucks, fire engines, planes, etc. I decided to try miniature renditions of these automotive creations. It was a fun-filled, relaxing project; once I got started it was difficult to stop.

### Feather Collage

Feathers not only make fine birds, but they can dress a miniature collage lady in her finest. The feathers are cut and shaped to resemble a garment and then glued onto a background. A head, feet and arms are added. If the dress is short, legs are included. Other feather cut-outs can become plants and foliage. Paper cut-outs are supplemental, and a thin line drawing finishes off the arrangement.

## Wood Collage

Get out those tiny scraps of wood you've been saving and make a collage out of assorted shapes and sizes. Use your leftover bits of dowel for small, flat round pieces. This is where your miter box is useful. Different color woods (mahogany, walnut, pine) can give interesting effects.

Glue your arrangement on a thin piece of cardboard, wood or Masonite, which can be left as is, painted, or covered with a textured surface of sandpaper or fabric.

## Ball Collage

This is a simple accumulation of four different sizes of beads.

Cut out cardboard (illustration board) 2" × 1¼". Using strips of

Fig. 4—10 Collages come in all shapes and forms. A feather-lady collage may tickle your fancy, or you may prefer the abstract ball collage. A wood collage on sandpaper background makes use of odd bits of various woods. The paper collage is made of printed material with overlays of torn colored tissue paper.

wood, make a simple box frame around this cardboard. Butt the sides against board and butt top and bottom against sides. Finished frame should jut forward from cardboard. Cover cardboard with thin layer of glue.

For placement of beads, start with one large bead about ¹/₄″ size. Using about four different and smaller sizes of beads, graduate their placement around and about the background.

Paint entire structure of beads, background and frame with white acrylic paint.

## Paper Collage

These are the types of collage most people are familiar with. You can use pictures from magazines or newspapers, prints of portraits and landscapes, fine art reproductions, tissue paper, wrapping paper and more. Combine several pictures, or make abstracts from colored paper. Keep in mind the scale of your rooms, and choose your material accordingly.

## FRAMES

Contemporary frames are basically simple. Traditional overtones may exist in certain styles, but for the most part they are lacking in ornamentation. Simple wood and metal frames are most commonly used. Some wood frames may be fastened together with a butt construction instead of the usual mitered corners.

For tabletop frames a piece of acrylic is molded into a structural shape (Fig. 4–12), easily accommodating a portrait, photograph or print.

## Frame A

A remarkable modern frame can be made for your prints, photographs, pastels and watercolors *if* the thickness of paper is confined to *less* than ¹/₃₂″.

The magic molding is Northeastern WS ³/₁₆″ and WS ¹/₈″ without recess. This window sash molding has a groove ready-made to receive your prints.

Measure your print. Plan and cut with an X-ACTO miter box the four WS sides necessary for the frame. Fit as you proceed. Be sure opposite sides match evenly for a perfectly squared frame.

Sand the four pieces and gently cut away any frayed edges.

Stain or paint the four pieces; let dry.

Glue three sides of frame together, positioning the wider section to the front.

Slip the print into the grooved areas. Try fourth side, and trim excess print if necessary. Glue fourth side at corners.

Fig. 4–11 An assortment of contemporary frames and pictures. Top left has four photos matted on one board and framed between two silver-painted moldings (Northeastern PFA-3). An Oriental watercolor painting is bordered with beige linen matting and white liner, with a thin gold-painted frame (Northeastern PFA-3). Left center is birds painted in acrylics on ceramic tiles, heavily framed in cherry. In the center, delicate lace on a dark blue background is framed in silver-painted Northeastern structural shape angle ⁵/₆₄″. Bottom left is a simple pen and ink drawing on light blue paper; the frame is swab sticks placed over cross-stitch mesh (Aida cloth) and painted cream color. At lower right Northeastern ¹/₈″ window sash molding is stained and placed around a picure cut from an advertising folder.

## Frame B

This double silver frame is the disposable structure that is used in plane models or car models to hold the working parts until ready to be structured. The little bumps at the center section of each four inner sides of "frame" will grab onto a thin cardboard mounted print that has been perfectly cut to fit the area. These structural shapes (once relieved of the inner working part) come in a variety of sizes. Inquire of someone who works with models.

**Frame C**

Another style frame can be made using the structural shape that model railroaders use—angles. There are metal angles and wooden angles of various sizes. The metal angles are strong and are cut with a file. The wooden angles are more fragile, and extra care should be used when cutting the corners with a sharp razor blade. Extra reinforcement is required in back. When painted silver or gold, it has a fine stream-lined look.

**Frame D**

The easiest method for a squared frame is the butt and glue technique. Miniaturists can control their own sizes for both molding and size of frame. The molding is simple strip wood. These frames are fine for accommodating anything from art to needlework. Stain or paint to personal tastes.

**Frame E**

A double bamboo frame uses $3/32''$ half-round molding from North-eastern. Cut a large rectangular shape from card. Cut out a center to frame your print. Cover card with fine material (silk, linen, colored cotton). Cut half-round molding for inner trim, mitering corners; incise even groove marks on trim; paint trim to match or contrast with material; glue trim down half on and half off edge. This provides a rabbet area. Leaving *even amount* of space all around, plan half-round molding for outside bamboo trim; miter corners; incise groove marks; color trim to match material; glue trim down. Cut away excess card along outside edges. Glue acetate-covered print or art work to frame.

**Frame F**

Strip of basswood (stained or painted) is made into a frame to surround a recessed piece of art board at least $1/16''$ thick. Art work is glued onto $1/16''$ block of basswood and adhered onto center portion of art board. Plan your own sizes and dimensions.

**Frame G**

Parallel strip moldings can be anything from Northeastern frame moldings to whatever is accommodating. The frame is merely two strips of molding glued to acetate matted prints for display. This method advantageously frames one or many prints all in one process.

**Frame H**

A clear photograph frame for a desk or table can be made from thin acrylic softened over heat and shaped into a position to hold a portrait. *Protection is necessary from direct heat of gas or electric.* Use a Flame Tamer on top of burner. Hold acrylic over Flame Tamer with tweezer or needle nose pliers. When it *begins* to soften, quickly remove

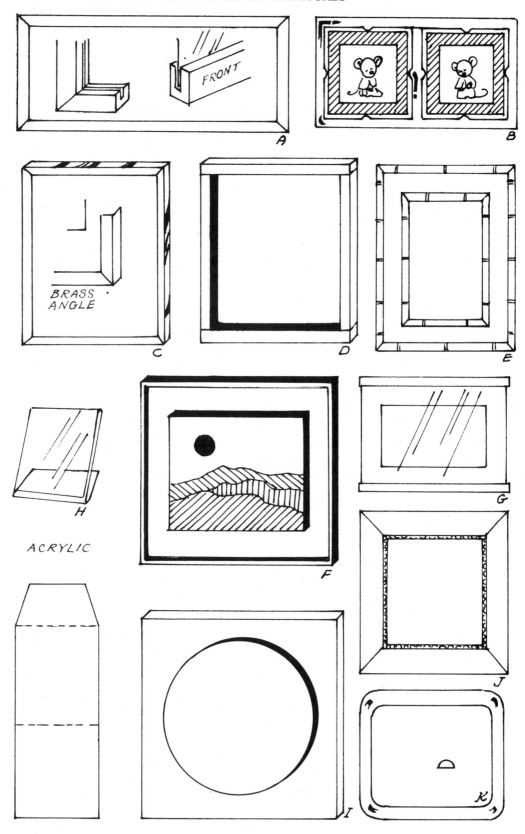

and insert kitchen knife, folding over on indicated dotted lines. Portraits are made from contact prints of a regular photograph.

### Frame I

Cut a section of square basswood (or other wood) $1/8''$ or less in thickness. Paint white. Cut perfect circle of $1/16''$ or less of wood. Paint a design on the circle and glue onto center of squared piece.

### Frame J

A wide frame is made from strip molding (basswood), mitered and glued together. Thin beading molding is measured, cut and glued to inside. Before gluing, beading molding is painted gold; wide outside molding is stained or painted.

### Frame K

A rounded frame takes time to sand for the finished effect. Rectangular shape of $1/8''$ basswood is cut. Outside corners are rounded. Inner area is cut out. Notice that inside corners are also rounded. The frame work is gently sanded so that entire top surface is rounded. When smoothly finished, paint white, black or a bright color. Spray with acrylic finish or use decoupage coating for satiny finish. Glue thin artwork to back.

Fig. 4–12 An assortment of framing techniques, which are described fully in text.

# 5

# Miniature Projects from Craft Supplies

## NEEDLEWORK MESH

Some miniaturists have already discovered the virtues of *needlepoint* and *latch-hook mesh.* For the uninitiated, this chapter will open up a new area of ideas.

Similar to felt materials, mesh can be moistened and molded into shape. Excess areas can be cut away without fraying, and edges can be joined together with glue. The mesh maintains firm shaping without having to paint on extra white glue for rigidity. If some meshes are of the soft variety (Aida cloth), then some extra gluing may be necessary.

The mesh is thoroughly moistened with water and then securely wrapped around an object of your choice. Glasses, bottles, bowls, and balls are all accommodating forms. The mesh is held tightly in place with rubber bands, tape, clips, plastic wrap or whatever is feasible. Fig. 8–8 in Chapter 8 shows mesh shaped between identical forms.

Since mesh lends itself so easily to cutting, gluing and shaping, it works into many architectural details, furniture and accessories. It can be painted any color.

Mesh can be used to simulate baskets, wicker furniture, or caning on chair seats. It can look light and airy, or have a heavier, woven texture.

*Note:* When planning a simulated "wicker" furnishing, try to match the natural color of wicker with acrylic paint. Some decorator wicker products are artificially colored with intense hues or painted white. These can be effective in the proper setting.

Fig. 5–2 shows a small sample of possible mesh creations. Other items could include wine racks; fern stand; telephone stand; bed tray;

Fig. 5–1 Different sizes of mesh prove useful in miniature work. Mono white interlock canvas has (A) 4 holes per inch; (B) 6 holes per inch; (D) 12 holes per inch and (E) 18 holes per inch. Penelope canvas, double mesh in (C) white and (F) tan. Aida cloth—a soft mesh used for counted cross-stitching—has (G) 14 threads per inch and (H) 11 threads per inch.

hamper; lamp shades; lamp bases; letter, napkin and tissue holders; luggage; trays and baskets for plants, flowers, hanging and shopping.

## Hanging Rattan Chair

### Materials

Needlepoint mesh mono white interlock canvas (6 holes per inch) for body of chair; double mesh small tan needlepoint mesh for seat; 3/8" wood (2" × 2"); white trim for edging; tacky glue (Velverette or other).

### Directions

1. Thoroughly wet mesh (A). Shake out excess water and wrap securely around baseball or ball of approximate size. Straighten out lines of mesh so they don't overlap and get stuck together. Wrap a piece of plastic wrap securely around mesh and ball. Secure with

paper clip (see Fig. 5–4). Slash a few holes in plastic to allow air to penetrate. Dry overnight.

2. Glue tan colored needlepoint mesh to top of seat (B).

3. Extra mesh was allowed on pattern A. Curved mesh will now be cut and shaped for chair. Before any cutting, apply white glue with fingers over the areas planned to be cut.

Study drawings to help decide where to cut. Notice that side view shows straight perpendicular sides. Measure from top to bottom. Cut away excess bottom. Left and right edges of mesh are determined by letters C and D on seat drawing.

4. When satisfied with shape, glue bottom of piece A to outer area of seat B.

5. Glue white trim or binding to edge of mesh.

6. Cover underside of seat with small needlepoint mesh. Stuff a little cotton between wood and mesh to create dropped-seat effect.

7. Glue trim around seat. An excellent choice is to cut a strip from the *edging* of the mesh.

8. Insert very small hook at center top; add a small coil of wire (from ball-point pen) and some chain.

Fig. 5–2 Needlework mesh, combined with wood, metal shapes and embroidery trims, can be turned into beautiful furnishings and accessories.

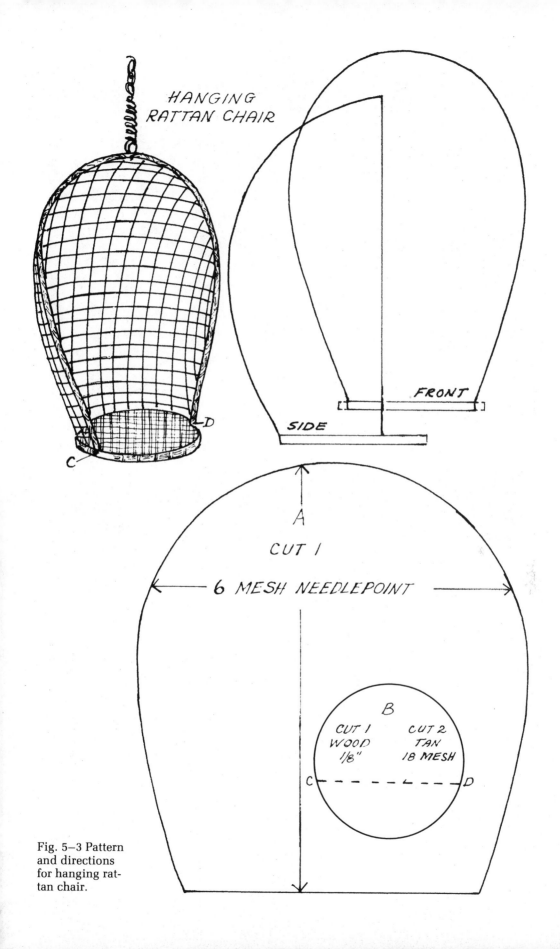

HANGING
RATTAN CHAIR

FRONT

SIDE

A

CUT 1

6 MESH NEEDLEPOINT

B

CUT 1
WOOD
1/8"

CUT 2
TAN
18 MESH

C ———————— D

C

D

Fig. 5–3 Pattern
and directions
for hanging rat-
tan chair.

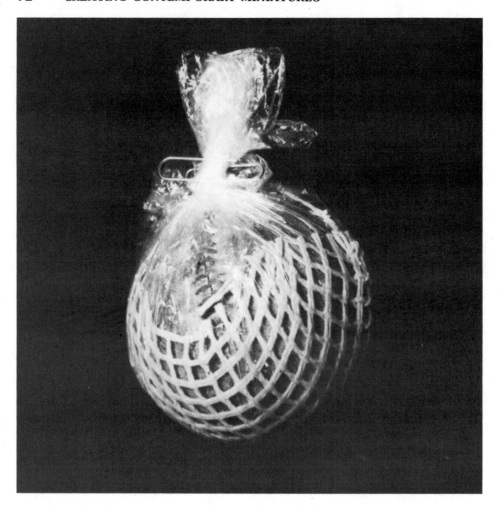

Fig. 5–4 To start the shaping for hanging rattan chair, the mesh is moistened with water and shaped around baseball or equivalent. Plastic wrap holds mesh securely until dry.

9. Mix "wicker" colored acrylic paint with white glue and brush over entire surface of mesh and seat.

### Cube Table

Round the corners of cube of wood. Measure around wood cube, and cut mesh to fit perfectly around four sides of cube. Paint mesh "wicker" color. Dry. Using glue, cover the cube with the wrap-around of colored mesh. Pull snugly; eliminate the showing of joined side as much as possible. Round corners of top piece B slightly. Glue B on top of cube.

Fig. 5–5 Pattern and directions for rattan cube table, folding screen and magazine rack.

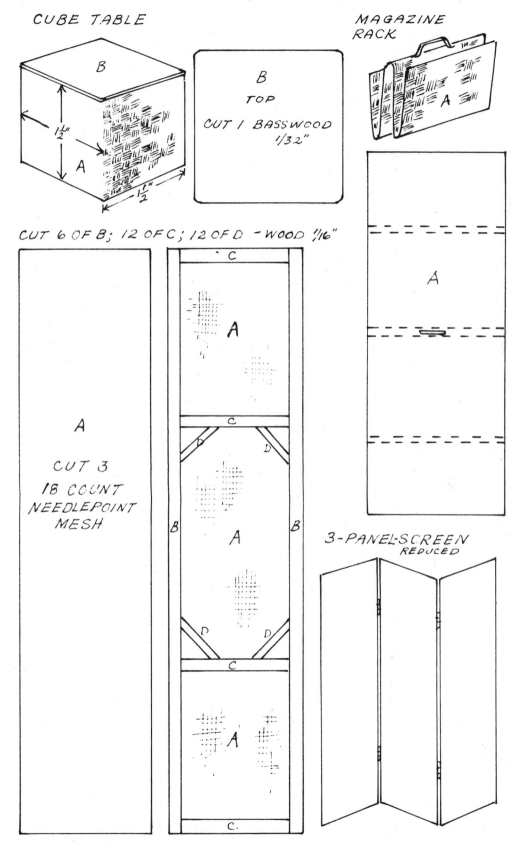

CUBE TABLE

MAGAZINE RACK

B

B
TOP
CUT 1 BASSWOOD
1/32"

A

1½"

A

1½"

CUT 6 OF B; 12 OF C; 12 OF D - WOOD 1/16"

A

CUT 3
18 COUNT
NEEDLEPOINT
MESH

C

A

C

D        D

A

B        B

A

D        D

C

A

C

A

3-PANEL SCREEN
REDUCED

## Magazine Rack

Cut-out of mesh piece is painted "wicker" color or gold on both sides. White glue is mixed with paint to give greater stiffness. Piece is folded back and forth using dotted lines as guide. Notice that dots allow for a squared edge at the three turnings. Add small strips of wood at turnings to reinforce each area if necessary. Curve and add a gold link handle to top center. Fill rack with "magazine covers" cut from subscription ads.

## Folding Screen

Three pieces of A are cut from 18-hole white interlock canvas. Paint mesh a light ochre. Pieces B, C, and D are cut from 1/16″ wood. Stain or paint wood.

Glue edge of A to piece B. Glue opposite edge of A to second piece B. Glue pieces C into position on mesh. Glue pieces D into position on mesh.

Repeat gluing for second and third panels. Hinge the panels together.

## Dried Plant Stand or Umbrella Stand

Glue four pieces of A together as shown in drawing. Cut small square of wood to fit within open bottom. Glue into place. Starting at a corner, glue cut and fitted mesh (Aida cloth) to four sides of stand. Cut 4 sections of brass angle (1/8″); each one to fit height of stand *plus* 1/8″ more for leg. Glue each corner piece into place. Trim top edge of stand with four strips of mesh, each carefully glued into place.

## Trash Basket

Curve mesh piece A into a tube and glue with a slight overlap of 1/8″. Cut a round of cardboard to fit bottom opening and glue into place. Starting at edge where mesh joins together, glue first swab stick piece B into place. Glue other three sticks equidistant from each other. Dry completely. Paint entire basket to match room decor. Note: This could also become a light fixture—as is, on a desk; or turned upside down as a ceiling fixture.

## Wall Panel

Cut a rectangle of 18 pt. tan mesh (double mesh). On top of mesh glue some embroidery or painted design. Using one pulled strand of mesh catch in holes on right and left top corners. Using glue, wind loose ends round and round. Clip excess. Add two tassels made from matching color sewing thread.

Fig. 5–6 Pattern parts and assembly for accessories: dried plant stand or umbrella stand, trash basket, wall panel, stationery holder, mirror and planter, and wall mirror.

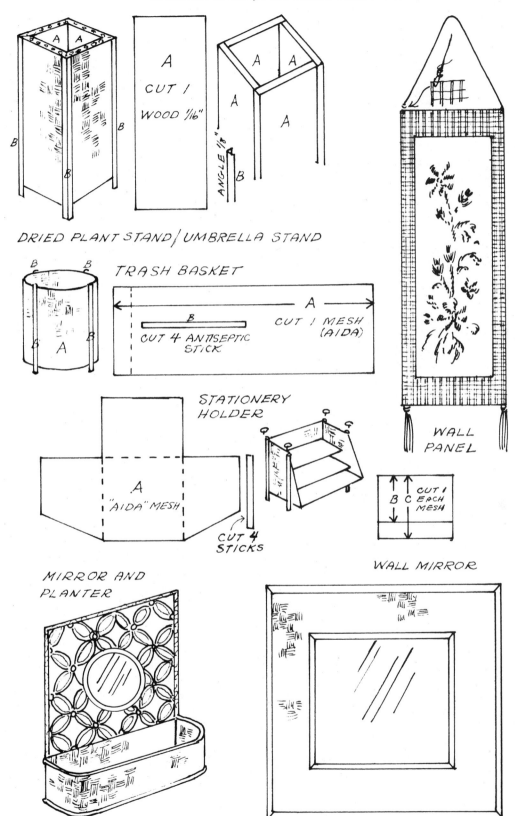

DRIED PLANT STAND / UMBRELLA STAND

A
CUT 1
WOOD 1/16"

ANGLE 1/8"

TRASH BASKET

A
CUT 1 MESH
(AIDA)

B
CUT 4 ANTISEPTIC
STICK

STATIONERY
HOLDER

A
"AIDA" MESH

CUT 4
STICKS

B C CUT 1
EACH
MESH

WALL
PANEL

WALL MIRROR

MIRROR AND
PLANTER

### Stationery Holder

Fold piece A indicated by dotted lines. Glue back corners together. Glue shelves Band C into position. Glue four swab sticks (legs) into position. Paint to match room decor. Four clipped pinheads can be glued onto top of each stick, if desired.

### Mirror and Planter

A special lace ribbon trim with flower design was selected for background piece. Round mirror ($3/4''$), purchased at craft shop, is glued in center. Mesh (Aida cloth) is used for bottom planter space, cut, shaped and glued into position. Cardboard is cut for bottom, fitted and glued to mesh. Edging of twine is added to top and bottom of planter, around mirror, and around three sides of back piece. Extra white glue was used in this project for greater stiffness.

### Wall Mirror

Needed: Square mirror; art board (depth of mirror); mesh (Aida cloth); half round $1/16''$; cardboard $2^{1}/_{2}'' \times 2^{1}/_{2}''$.

In center of art board cut out hole the same size as mirror. Glue both mirror and art board to cardboard. Carefully glue cut mesh to art board surrounding mirror. Cut half round for inner and outer framing, mitering the corners. Paint half rounds white, and glue onto mesh.

## NATURE'S BOUNTY

Sometimes we take nature for granted. But it's all around us, and a contemporary decor can make marvelous use of bits and pieces as decorative accessories.

The beach yields seashells, driftwood and small eroded stones. Stones from riverbeds are often rounded and smooth. In the fall there are many beautiful dried flowers and grasses.

### Seashells

Shells up to one inch in size can be displayed as art objects or can be put to use as plant holders, lamp bases, bookends, and serving pieces. Smaller shells can be worked into any number of decorative arrangements including flowers, candles, ships, dolls, animals, and birds. A collection can be displayed in a drum table as shown in chapter 11 (Fig. 11–9).

### Minerals

Tiny chips of amethyst, turquoise, malachite or others can be set up as a unique hobby collection, or one single mineral can be displayed within a capsule or dome, small or large.

### Seeds

Small seeds can be dried out and made into a beautiful mosaic for a wall or under a glass-topped table, or can be transformed into flowers

Fig. 5–7 Nature's wonders make surprisingly beautiful art objects in contemporary settings. One rock, left side, resembles a monkey; other rocks are eroded with beautiful shapes that resemble sculpture. Gnarled wood (center) becomes a table base. A piece of ebony wood resembles two figures. Seashell birds sit upon a "log." A large piece of coral (top center) would make a superlative background for plant material. The cat is a piece of wood with a knothole eye.

Fig. 5–8 Macrame beads come in many sizes, shapes and beautiful colors.

as in chapter 11 (Fig. 11–13). The seeds can be left in their natural brown and yellow colors, or they can be painted.

### Grasses and Flowers

These can be dried in silica gel or pressed flat for arrangements. Placed between two thin pieces of acrylic, the pressed flowers can be placed in windows, or made into folding screens.

### Wood

Twigs become "logs" and are used as fireplace logs and pedestals. A large half-log can be turned into a bench with log legs, and bowls can be crudely fashioned from a small cutting. Delicate stems and branches placed within a large floor "pot" look strikingly like a stripped tree. Little pieces of driftwood can be individually displayed, or used with a plant arrangement. Driftwood also makes a lovely base for stone sculpture.

### Stone

Rocks and pebbles become useful backgrounds for fireplaces, indoor ponds and fountain constructions. Tiny, tiny pebbles can be made into rock people and rock pets. The ocean throws up some interesting formations of worn rocks and broken seashells, which can be used as modern sculptures. Flattened thin stones become excellent base pieces.

## MACRAME BEADS

It's very comforting to have macrame as an ongoing hobby along with miniaturing. There is a wide, beautiful, glorious selection of macrame beads, and countless ways to use them.

Sizes range from very small to very large, and shapes, colors, finishes and designs are too numerous to describe.

Vases seem to be the most popular use for beads, but the larger ones (especially ceramic ones with holes of ½" or more) make very

Fig. 5–9 The tiniest of pom-poms are made into precious little toy animals of cats, ducks, rabbits and teddy bears. Kitty McKenna had fun fitting them all together in assorted ways and colors. Bead eyes, felt ears and yarn ties help make them lovable.

Fig. 5–10 Men's ties come in a wide variety of patterns and textures that can be useful in miniaturing.

impressive floor planters. These same ceramic beads become wonderful hanging light fixtures with a few extra attachments (see Fig. 1–13). Another type can be glued to the ceiling for a spotlight style. Some can be used singly or in stacks as table lampbases.

Large beads can become pedestals for art work, bases for small or large tables, or stools when topped with small pillows.

## POM-POMS

Pom-poms started out big, but they've been getting smaller and smaller, which makes them useful for the miniaturist. They do work up into darling cuddly soft animals, but pom-poms can be used in wall decorations, too. Children's rooms, powder rooms and theme rooms can best benefit from this novel approach. Three-dimensional designs take shape in potted plants, flowers or trees, and realism is sacrificed for whimsy and fun. Pom-poms can be used to decorate a store window and can become great holiday decorations.

## NECKTIES

Men's ties lend themselves very nicely to miniature work, since their various designs and textures are often on a small scale. Silk materials are most in demand, but ties of rayon, wool and cotton are also desirable and usable. There are textures, embossed patterns, prints, brocades, solids, stripes and weaves.

Some rather elegant doll's clothing can be made from selective designs. A lady's formal gown can benefit from a fine silk material, and a small brocade ends up as a man's smoking jacket or formal jacket. Other wearing apparel depends upon design and weight of material. There are some ties that would make nice tablecloths or placemats, and others that might be suitable for covering a lambrequin. Some modern designs are wonderful for contemporary upholstered furniture.

# Part II

## Miniature Rooms and Shops

# INTRODUCTION

THIS section is pure enjoyment for me, because it not only involves creating some new furnishings, but also putting them together and seeing a finished room. I'm sure that all miniaturists share this feeling of accomplishment.

The initial idea for a room may grab hold at any unexpected moment, but then how to get started? Take your time and do a little research. Make full use of any local libraries and museums. Do sketches and drawings; take measurements of actual furnishings.

Once you have gathered your information, the building process begins. It is usually helpful to draw full-size floor and wall layouts. These can be taped together for a three-dimensional effect. Windows, doors or any built-in structures should be penciled in to check on sizing. If purchased furnishings and accessories are already available, which is often the case, these should be placed on the paper layouts to make sure everything will fit. Many rooms are designed around the major furnishings.

Through text and photographs the following chapters will show how some of my rooms and furnishings were made. No room is meant to be copied exactly, but feel free to borrow or rearrange ideas to suit your own needs.

# 6

# Oriental World

STARTING a new room can sometimes be a tormenting decision. My incentive is there; my ideas are bubbling over, and ten fingers are itching to begin. At first I thought I'd toss all my ideas into a hat and pull out the lucky winner (idea) for a decisive beginning. Instead, I pulled out my boxes of stored miniatures, and after looking through them, I realized there was an abundance of Oriental items. I must have known that I would someday make an Oriental room; why else would I have collected and made so many attractive miniatures of Eastern origin? The subconscious desire was apparent, and my decision was made.

## BOX CONSTRUCTION AND FINISHING

The box for this room is 20″ wide, 12″ deep and 12″ high.

### Directions

1. Sections for the basic box are cut out of ¼″ plywood or wood of your choice. All surfaces should be sanded. Window opening is cut out of back. The sides and floor are glued and nailed together, but the top is left off until later.

2. The door is constructed from ¹⁄₁₆″ plywood (obtained from model hobby shop), ¹⁄₃₂″ sheet basswood, cut into strips, and door molding. Paint or stain, and set aside.

3. The corner platform is constructed of ¼″ balsa wood or heavy cardboard, with a diagonal step at one corner (see Fig. 6–2). Small

Fig. 6–1 This Oriental shop is resplendent with green and gold wallpaper, red carpeting and a varied selection of merchandise. Some of the items were purchased, while others are jewelry remnants.

Fig. 6–2 Platform is constructed from ¼" wood, with small blocks of wood placed underneath. Top surface and step are covered with red velvet.

blocks of wood are glued underneath. The platform is covered with carpeting, in this case, red velvet.

Two half walls are constructed and glued to each side near the step. These walls can be made to suit individual tastes. The walls in my room started with two carved ivory pocketbook handles, purchased

Fig. 6–3 The finished room before furnishings are added.

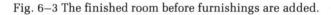

Fig. 6–4 Ivory pocketbook handles become perfect ornate tops for wall dividers covered with needlepoint mesh. Polished stones are made into collages and framed with hair barrettes. The pottery pieces on the left were purchased at a garden shop, and the large carved ivory fisherman was found at an antique show.

at an antique show long ago. These were glued to the top edge of 1/8″ pieces of pine, which were covered on the outside with tan 18-mesh needlepoint canvas. The insides were covered with the same covering as the walls of room.

Another small raised area was made from a 1/2″ × 2″ block of balsa wood (see Fig. 6–3 and 6–7). The length is cut to fit snugly against the wall under the window, and is covered with matching carpeting (red velvet). The entire platform is glued into place after the floor has been laid and the walls finished.

4. The wall covering is glued onto the sides of box. Allow an extra 1/4″ of covering on side walls to extend onto back wall. Glue back wall covering last. Use wallpaper paste or white glue, diluted slightly with water. Apply adhesive with flat edge brush; lay paper or fabric covering onto wall, and carefully push air bubbles out. My covering is a green and gold, commercial wallpaper that I found at a local store several years ago. I liked it and thought "Someday there will be a use for it."

5. The flooring is laid. The one in my room is a Handley House floor consisting of various strips of veneer randomly glued to paper backing. Most of the floor can be conveniently glued down as one

Fig. 6–5 The window frame was made from a microscope slide tray that was cut down to four sections. The Oriental design was painted with watercolors on rice paper.

piece. Since the box is wider than the flooring, the extra area is covered with flooring that is not used under the platform area.

6. The window structure is the result of a generous gift from an acquaintance who gave me several microscope slide trays. These wooden trays usually hold six slides but for this room I modified a tray to four sections, removed the old paper and painted the wood with black acrylic. White rice paper was cut to fit, and Oriental designs, carefully and lightly drawn onto the paper, were rendered with watercolors. The paper was glued to the back of the tray frame.

Rice paper is exquisite. When a light is placed in back of the painted area, a beautiful luminous quality shines through. But extra precautions are needed when transporting a box with an exterior rice-paper window, as the paper is very fragile. When traveling, carefully tape a protective piece of cardboard onto the outside wall.

Moldings are necessary to finish off the window edges. Before the window is glued into place, cut and miter a set of moldings for both the inside and outside of the window. These should slightly overlap both window and wall areas to conceal the joints. The molding used here was Northeastern CRA-6.

Paint the inside molding black. Stain or paint the outside molding to match the outside walls. Glue the window frame into place, then

Fig. 6–6 The room has elephants carved out of wood, ivory and bone. Most of the wall accessories are jewelry pieces. The horses are Chinese paper cuttings by Cheng Ho-Tien. The see-through block structure contains a beautiful hand-carved cork scene. The brass incense burner is an impressive piece in front of a Petite Princess screen.

carefully glue molding around window inside and outside.

7. Place finished door and glue into position. Turn the box so the rear wall is on the table and place a weight on door until dried. If desired, add extra Oriental ornamentation around doorway, and purchased door hardware.

8. Finish the ceiling with white paint or wall paper. Attach an Oriental light fixture.

9. Glue and nail the top onto box.

10. Finish the exterior to your personal tastes.

11. Box may have a glass or acrylic front if desired.

12. Glue all accessories and furnishings in place.

Fig. 6–7 A closer view of the platform area shows pottery, carved coral, dried arrangements, brick-a-brac and trinkets. The artwork is by the author.

## FLOOR DISPLAY STAND

### *Materials*

A sheet of ⅛″ pine or basswood; jar of red acrylic paint.

### *Directions*

1. Sand all pieces, keeping edges and corners sharp.
2. Glue piece A to piece B.
3. Glue piece C to piece B. Set aside.
4. Glue piece D to piece E. Set aside.
5. Repeat process for other side.
6. Paint pieces A through E plus lower top, bright red or color of your choice.
7. When paint is dry, glue pieces D to pieces C.

Fig. 6–8 Patterns and assembly guide for floor display stand, plant stand and base for art objects.

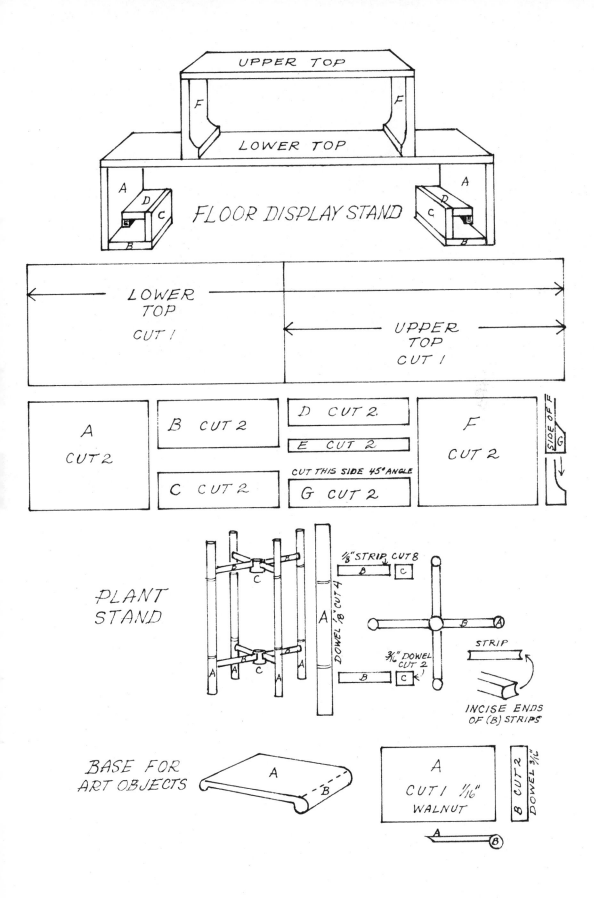

UPPER TOP

F · F

LOWER TOP

A · A

D · D
C · C
E · B
B · B

FLOOR DISPLAY STAND

LOWER
TOP
CUT 1

UPPER
TOP
CUT 1

A
CUT 2

B CUT 2

C CUT 2

D CUT 2.

E CUT 2

CUT THIS SIDE 45° ANGLE

G CUT 2

F
CUT 2

SIDE OFF
G

PLANT
STAND

B · B
C
A · A · C · A · A

DOWEL ⅛" CUT 4
A

⅛" STRIP CUT 8
B · C

B · A

3/16" DOWEL
CUT 2
B · C

STRIP

INCISE ENDS
OF (B) STRIPS

BASE FOR
ART OBJECTS

A
B

A
CUT 1 11/16"
WALNUT

B CUT 2
DOWEL 3/16"

A · B

Fig. 6–9 The floor display stand shows off art objects, and the plant stand can hold baskets or urns. The tall, white ceramic figure was a garden shop purchase, and the carved lamp finial (left) becomes a lovely "sculptured" decoration.

8. Glue top edges of side pieces A to lower top.

9. Top section: Glue pieces G to pieces F as shown. Allow to dry, then using chisels and needle file, shape G until rounded as shown in Fig. 6–8.

10. Glue pieces F to upper top.

11. Paint remaining pieces bright red or color of your choice, and allow to dry thoroughly.

12. Center and glue two sections together. Touch up painted areas where necessary.

*Note:* With different dimensions, either of these sections could become a cocktail table, bench or other furnishing.

## PLANT STAND

### *Materials*
Dowels ⅛″ and ³/₁₆″; ⅛″ strip of pine, basswood or spruce.

### *Directions*
1. Score each dowel A as shown in Fig. 6–8 to simulate bamboo.

2. Using rattail needle file, incise the ends of strips B as shown.

3. Glue two strips B to dowel A as shown. When dry, glue other end of strips to dowels C.

4. Repeat step 3 on other three legs, drying thoroughly between each leg.

5. Paint stand desired color.

Fig. 6–10 An Oriental table made from cherry wood holds a pair of lamps with coral bead bases. The shades are tan rice paper trimmed with gold paper. On the floor is a mother-of-pearl pin. The Ming-style rug is made from tan cashmere material, with the design done with a blue marking pen. The plant stand holds a basket made from needlepoint mesh.

## BASE FOR ART OBJECTS

### *Materials*
Walnut wood $^1/_{16}$"; dowel $^3/_{16}$"; walnut stain.

### *Directions*
1. Incise a circular edging on both sides of piece A to accommodate dowel pieces B.
2. Stain dowels B to match A.
3. Glue B to A. Dry thoroughly. Sand any irregularities until smooth. Repeat staining where necessary.

*Note:* Bases can be painted black instead of stained.

## ORIENTAL TABLE

### *Materials*
Cherry wood or other hardwood: $^1/_{16}$", $^1/_8$", $^1/_4$"; wood glue (Titebond or other).

### *Directions*
1. Sand each piece carefully. Check fit. Apply clear finish of your choice, and allow to dry.
2. Centering, glue piece B to underside of piece A. Use rubber bands or small clamps to hold together until dry.
3. On underside of B, glue one leg piece C in position as shown by dotted lines. Use triangle to obtain straight lineup.
4. Glue crosspiece D next to and flush with attached leg C on underside of piece B. Place other crosspiece on opposite side in same position.
5. Glue other leg piece C into position.
6. Glue pieces E into position.
7. Glue pieces F into position.
8. Pieces C, D, E and F should be flush on front. If necessary, sand until smooth and touch-up finish.

*Note:* If pine or basswood is used, a stain should be applied. The table can also be painted, lacquered and hand-painted with designs.

## MING DESIGN CARPET

### *Materials*
Tan cashmere fabric; blue color permanent marking pen.

### *Directions*
Transfer design to fabric and paint over with marking pen. Add a fringe at two ends if desired.

Fig. 6–11 Patterns and assembly guide for Oriental table, and Ming design rug.

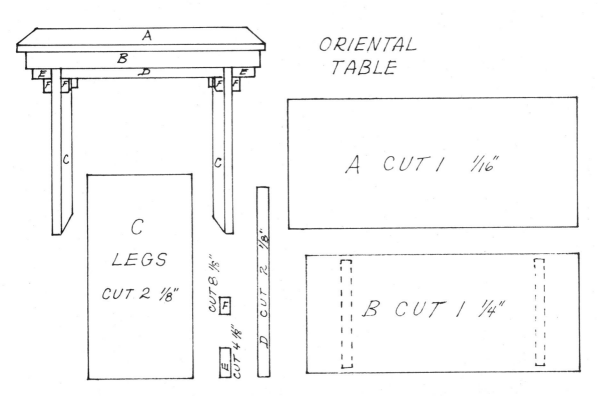

ORIENTAL
TABLE

A

B

E D E

F F F F

C C

C

LEGS

CUT 2 ⅛"

CUT 8 ½"

F

E

CUT 4 ⅛"

D CUT 2 ⅛"

A CUT 1 ¹⁄₁₆"

B CUT 1 ¼"

MING DESIGN RUG

# 7

# Contemporary Bedroom

SOMETIMES rooms just happen! This bedroom came into being because the fabric proved to be an irresistable purchase. The fabric's tiny flowers are blue, rose and mustard yellow on a white background. There were other materials readily at hand, so a new room was started.

The carpet is dark blue velvet, and the armchair is covered with gold velvet. The woodwork is painted French blue, and other blue accents show up in ruffled pillow shams and the Hollywood phone. The table-desk has brass trim, and the classic Parsons bed and desk chair are upholstered in Haitian cotton. The contemporary dresser and bedside table add warm tones of cherry wood.

The construction starts with a basic box 16″ wide, 12″ deep and 12″ high. I believe that bedrooms should provide a place for quiet retreat and privacy, so I included furnishings for reading and writing.

The step-up layout adds interest and provides extra storage space (faked) with drawers finished off in the same floral print used on walls and comforter. The lower level is 3½″ deep. A dramatic effect is created by massive amounts of drapery shirred across the back wall, extending from floor to ceiling. Clothes hanger wire is used at top and bottom and is held in place with eye screws at each end. To prevent wire from bending, nails are driven through material at center of top and bottom. The louvered doors on the left were purchased.

## UPHOLSTERED CHAIR

### Materials

Wood 1/16″, 1/8″, 1/4″, pine or basswood; material for upholstery; matching embroidery floss or crochet yarn; art foam; foam for seat cushion.

Fig. 7–1 A beautiful floral material was the starting point of this bedroom with two-level flooring. The latch hook wall hanging was made by Meg Nyberg. In foreground, two antique ceramic swans add aesthetic interest.

### Directions

1. Soak back piece C in boiling water. When softened, curve piece around small glass or jar with 2″ diameter. Secure tightly with rubber bands. Dry overnight.

2. Side pieces D can be slightly curved on angled side where arrow points in same manner.

3. Glue top base piece B onto base piece A. Center B on A with front edges flush. (see Fig. 7–7 and 7–8).

4. Glue back piece C to rabbet area of base pieces A and B. Allow to dry.

5. If side pieces D were curved, glue entire piece against back piece C and along bottom rabbet area of A and B. Repeat for other side. If the pieces were not curved, glue only diagonal sides of piece D against back piece. When thoroughly dry, force side piece into place and glue.

Fig. 7–2 Side walls are covered first, with fabric extending onto back wall. An extra covering is also added to top area of back wall. Platform is set on blocks of wood, which are glued into place.

Fig. 7–3 Carpeting is glued down on both floor areas. Extend carpet over front edge of upper area. Small simulated drawers covered with matching wall pattern are glued to front panel. The step is a small balsa block covered with carpet material.

Fig. 7–4 A close-up of the writing area showing simulated wicker accessories and other incidentals. The hanging lamp is made of white plastic curtain rings, lamp check ring and coiled wire. The dark blue macrame wall hanging was made by Marilyn Diesu. The metal Goddess of Fertility standing below the hanging was brought back from the island of Crete, a gift from my sister-in-law, Evelyn.

    6. Sand joined areas smooth,

    7. On bottom of base piece A, drill or rout out four holes (tooth-pick size) for pegs of chair legs.

    8. Repeat routing on tops of chair legs.

    9. Sand and stain leg pieces J and K. Insert and glue toothpick pegs into legs. See Fig. 7–7 for placement. Set legs aside until later.

Fig. 7–5 The right side of the room features cherry wood furnishings with working drawers. A tri-view mirror rests on the dresser, and an attractive gold velvet chair provides reading comfort.

## Chair Upholstery

Always check pattern against wooden shell of chair to be sure of proper fit. Sometimes adjustments are necessary, especially if different thicknesses of fabric are used. Cut and adjust as you work.

Apply small, even amounts of tacky glue to wrong side of material on cutting edge of pattern before cutting. Allow to dry. This glue prevents fraying.

Keep clean water and a clean, damp cloth nearby for cleaning up glue spills on upholstery.

Do not apply glue to entire surface of foam. If you do, it will produce a hard surface.

### Directions

1. Spot-glue (with white tacky glue) piece of art foam E to inner back and side of chair frame. If small amount of foam extends beyond edge, do not trim; it will soften edging as upholstery is pulled over it.

Fig. 7–6 Pattern and assembly guide for upholstered armchair.

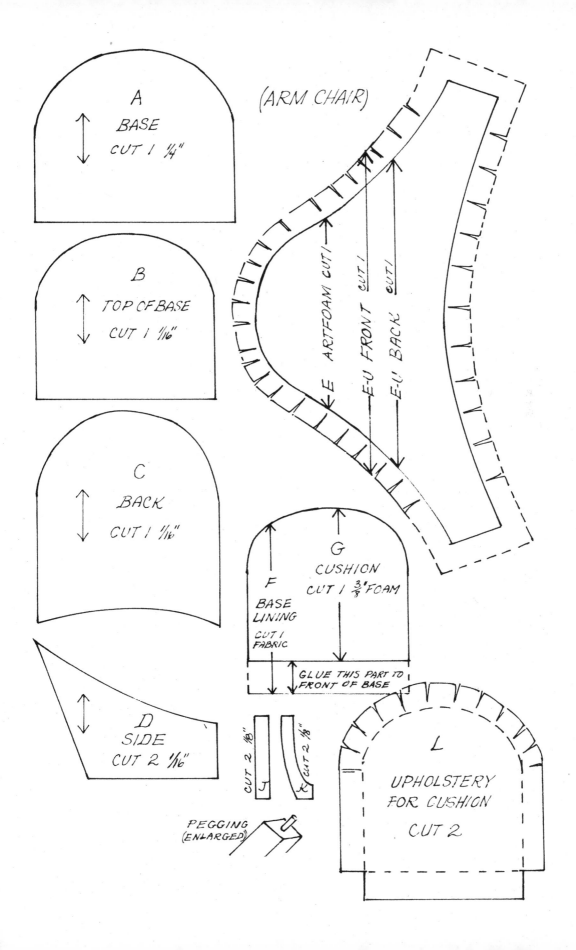

(ARM CHAIR)

A
BASE
CUT 1 ¼"

B
TOP OF BASE
CUT 1 ¹⁄₁₆"

C
BACK
CUT 1 ¹⁄₁₆"

D
SIDE
CUT 2 ¹⁄₁₆"

E   ARTFOAM CUT 1
E-U FRONT CUT 1
E-U BACK CUT 1

F
BASE
LINING
CUT 1
FABRIC

G
CUSHION
CUT 1 ⅜" FOAM

GLUE THIS PART TO
FRONT OF BASE

J   CUT 2 ⅛"
K   CUT 2 ⅛"

PEGGING
(ENLARGED)

L
UPHOLSTERY
FOR CUSHION
CUT 2

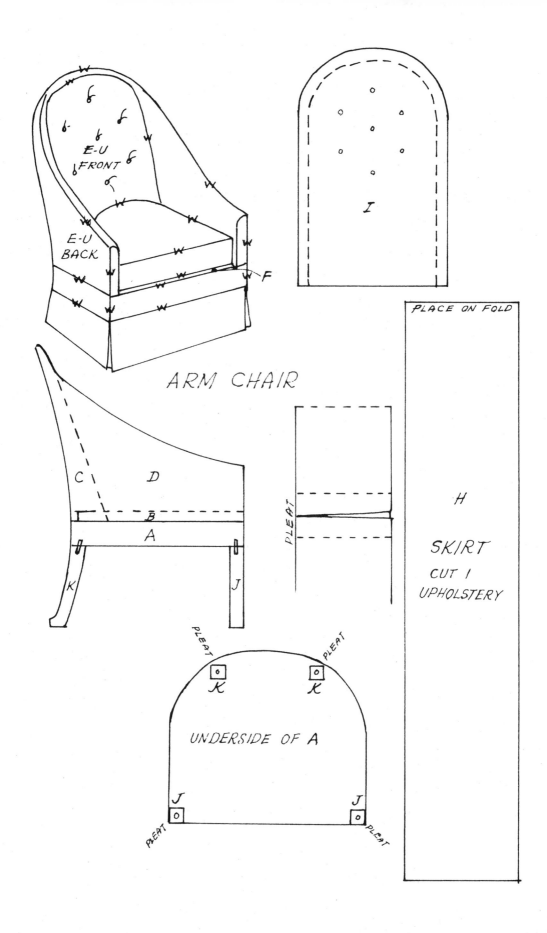

E-U
FRONT

E-U
BACK

F

ARM CHAIR

I

C   D

B

A

K        J

PLEAT

PLACE ON FOLD

H

SKIRT

CUT 1

UPHOLSTERY

PLEAT        PLEAT

K        K

UNDERSIDE OF A

J        J

PLEAT        PLEAT

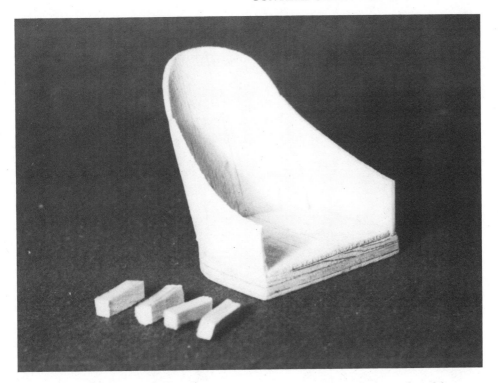

Fig. 7–8 The wooden structure of the armchair is ready to be upholstered, and four legs are ready to be shaped.

2. Apply tacky glue to bottom edge (wrong side) of upholstery piece EU front. Starting at center bottom on base A gently press material along base edge. Tap into place with tweezers. Let dry. Gently pull upholstery up and *over* inner surface of chair to back. Glue edges to back of chair (see Fig. 7–9). If necessary, trim away any excess material at corner while being stretched around *front* arm area to side.

3. Glue base lining piece F into place extending down front of chair. Clip where necessary.

4. Starting at center top back, carefully glue upholstery back piece EU into place. Gently pull material to cover back surface of chair. Cut off excess at front by arm, if necessary.

5. Skirt of chair: With opening at back, mark four inverted pleats located at two front corners (J) and at two back legs (K). Press pleats with iron; add a little glue at top. Set aside.

6. Back cushion: With right sides together, stitch two pieces of I, leaving bottom open. Clip edges, and turn right side out. Insert art foam cut to fit. With one strand of embroidery floss or crochet yarn, sew French knots as indicated on Fig. 7–7. Edge top and sides with

Fig. 7–7 Pattern and assembly guide (continued) for upholstered armchair.

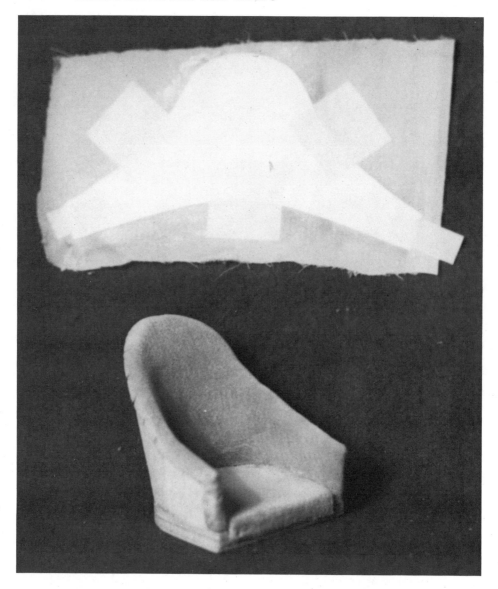

Fig. 7–9 Paper pattern is taped to fabric for cutting. The base has EU front piece and F piece applied.

same floss or yarn. Trim bottom and glue to (inner) back portion of chair.

    7. Attach legs of chair to underside in positions shown on pattern. Legs should be pegged with toothpicks to underside for greater strength.

    8. Seat cushion covering: Spot-glue sides of one piece L to all sides of foam cushion. Turn over. Spot-glue sides of second piece L.

Fig. 7–10 Pattern and assembly guide for classic Parsons bed.

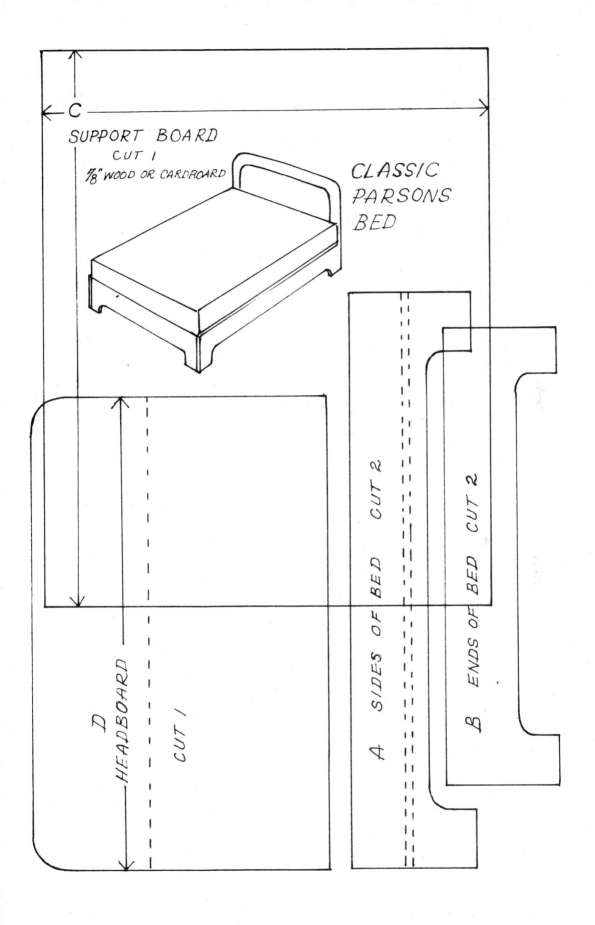

SUPPORT BOARD
CUT 1
7/8" WOOD OR CARDBOARD

CLASSIC
PARSONS
BED

C

D HEADBOARD
CUT 1

A SIDES OF BED CUT 2

B ENDS OF BED CUT 2

Fig. 7–11 Base of bed with rounded corners and foam in cavity. Second rectangle of foam is cut for mattress.

Sides will now glue on *top* of first fabric covering. Clip around back curve where necessary.

9. Apply tacky glue to upper part of skirt and press into position.

10. Welting: Glue embroidery floss or crochet yarn onto edges for welting. It is indicated by W on Fig. 7–7.

## CLASSIC PARSONS BED

### Materials for Base

Wood—pine or basswood 1/8", or very thick cardboard; fabric for upholstery; foam for mattress and spring.

### Directions

1. Glue side pieces A and end pieces B to edge of support board piece C. Dotted lines on A in Fig. 7–10 show placement. Add glue to edge corners of A and B for firm hold. Dry completely and sand corners round.

2. Cut piece of foam to fit within cavity area of bed. Spot-glue to support board.

3. Starting with side areas, cover the base with fabric that has been cut 1/2" larger than pattern. Cut away where necessary to fit around legs

Fig. 7–12 Each side of bed has upholstery piece cut ¹/₂″ larger for fold-over. Fabric is glued under as shown.

but extend fabric to underside of bed and around legs to end sections and up over onto foam at least ¹/₂″ (see Fig. 7–12). All side areas will be covered.

4. Repeat same fabric covering with ends of bed, mitering the corners this time.

5. Cut a piece of fabric 4⁵/₈″ × 5³/₄″. Center over top of bed and glue firmly around edges, covering foam and raw edges of previously upholstered areas.

6. Cut another section of foam ¹/₂″ deep for mattress, and cover with white sheeting or material of your choice.

7. Make two pillows and dress rest of bed according to your tastes. Since it is an upholstered base, the most appropriate covering is a comforter that tucks under the mattress. Pillow coverings in my room are ruffled shams, and the comforter matches the wall covering.

### Upholstered Headboard for Parsons Bed

#### *Materials*

Heavy cardboard or ¹/₈″ wood cut 3¹/₂″ × 5″; upholstery fabric; white sheeting or muslin, cotton batting (two layers).

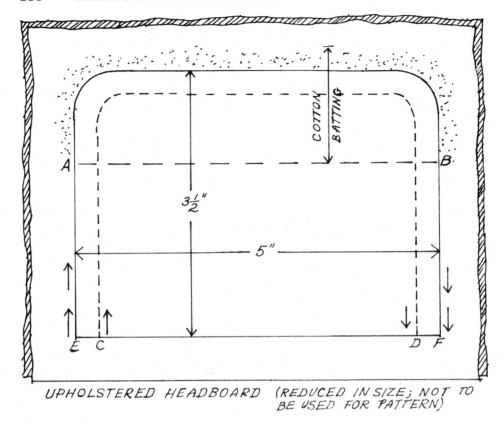

COTTON BATTING

$3\frac{1}{2}''$

$5''$

A                                                                    B

E  C                                                        D  F

UPHOLSTERED HEADBOARD (REDUCED IN SIZE; NOT TO BE USED FOR PATTERN)

Fig. 7–13 Assembly guide for upholstered headboard for bed.

### Directions

1. Round the two top corners of board D.

2. Draw pencil line across board about 1¼" down (see Fig. 7–13 from A to B). Set aside.

3. Cut both fabrics all around at least 1" larger in area than board.

4. With cotton sheeting or muslin underneath upholstery fabric, stitch or sew from A to B (see Fig. 7–14) through both fabrics approximating where drawn line would be.

5. Cut enough cotton batting to fit into top area, allowing an extra ¼" batting around sides and top. Extra will be pushed under for puffier outside roll.

6. Lightly apply pencil line in U-shape from C to D. Stitch on line.

7. Stuff extra cotton batting under, close to stitched line, and stitch in U-shape from E to F.

8. Carefully cut away white cotton sheeting close to E-F stitching.

9. Place upholstered piece on board, pull edges tightly to back, and glue.

10. Cut piece of upholstery fabric to cover back and glue down.

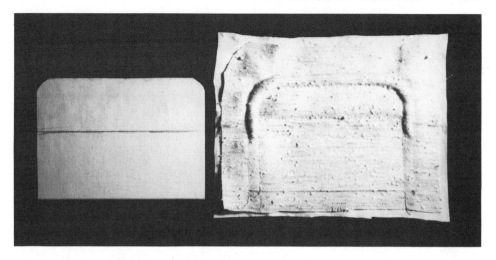

Fig. 7–14 The wood or heavy cardboard (left) is cut out for headboard. On right, the puffed material before sheeting to trimmed.

## DRESSER

This piece can be used in a dining room, living room or studio apartment. It can be made with light or dark woods and finished in different ways. The drawer fronts can be covered with fine needlepoint mesh for a "cane look"; half-round moldings can be added; scored lines can be incised; Formica can be substituted.

Fig. 7–15 A bedside table and dresser made from cherry wood. The beautiful grain is retained on the drawer fronts. The tri-view mirror uses Northeastern frame molding and H hinges. A boxbag rests on the gold velvet armchair.

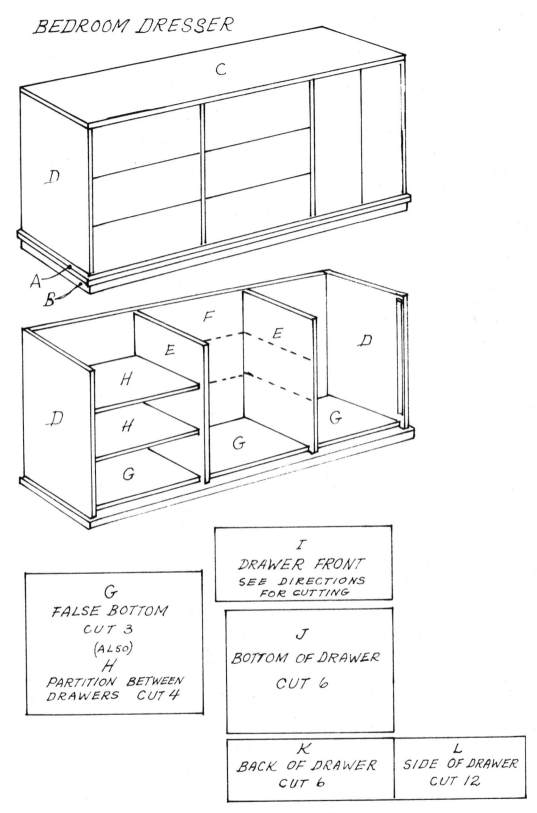

# BEDROOM DRESSER

**C**

**D**

**A**

**B**

**F**

**E**

**E**

**D**

**H**

**D**

**H**

**G**

**G**

**G**

**G**

| I |
|---|
| DRAWER FRONT |
| SEE DIRECTIONS |
| FOR CUTTING |

| G |
|---|
| FALSE BOTTOM |
| CUT 3 |
| (ALSO) |
| H |
| PARTITION BETWEEN |
| DRAWERS CUT 4 |

| J |
|---|
| BOTTOM OF DRAWER |
| CUT 6 |

| K | L |
|---|---|
| BACK OF DRAWER | SIDE OF DRAWER |
| CUT 6 | CUT 12 |

Fig. 7–16 Pattern and assembly guide for bedroom dresser.

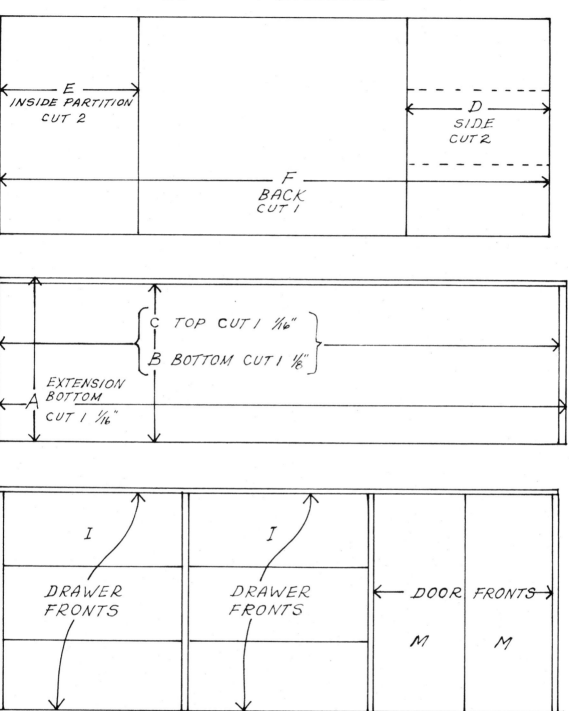

Fig. 7–17 Pattern and assembly guide (continued) for bedroom dresser.

The beauty of the piece in my room is in the continuous wood grain design on the drawer front and doors. To be perfectly matched, each group of three drawers is cut out of one piece of wood to assure perfect alignment. A well-grained wood is recommended. Special caution should be taken when cutting the drawer pieces, so that minimal filing is necessary.

Before you have finished, the drawers will be in and out of the frame dozens of times. To facilitate proper placement write a penciled number on the insides of drawer fronts 1, 2, 3, 4, 5, 6 starting at left top. Also write an arrow pointing downward to indicate direction of fit.

### Materials

Hardwood; all pieces are cut from $1/16''$ thickness except for bottom piece B which is $1/8''$ thickness. Measure! Be sure pieces D, E, and F are all the same height before gluing together.

### Directions

1. Glue side pieces D to back piece F. Use 90° triangle to assure straight alignment (see Fig. 7–18).

2. Glue bottoms of pieces D and F to extended bottom piece A. Extension is in front and on sides; backs should be flush.

3. Glue one false bottom G into left side.

4. Glue first inside partition E into place. To be sure of fit and straight alignment, take one drawer front I and slide up and down *before* glue sets.

Fig. 7–18 When gluing furniture together, line up a 90° angle by using a triangle.

Fig. 7–19 The framework of the dresser with lines drawn for placement of drawer partitions.

5. Glue center false bottom piece G into place.

6. Glue second inside partition E into place.

7. Glue third false bottom into place.

8. Glue structure onto base bottom B. A overlaps B on front and sides, but is flush in the back.

**Drawers**

1. Construct bottom left drawer (#3) first. Glue two side pieces L to bottom piece J and back piece K to sides and bottom piece.

2. Glue front piece I to above structure. Top of drawer is level. Bottom front will extend $1/16''$ below. Let dry.

3. Partition piece H will be glued into proper place above drawer. Try partition for snug fit. Drawer should still pull in and out easily. Mark with pencil. When satisfied, remove drawer and glue partition H into place. Keep drawer in place *only* until you're sure of fit. Allow partition to dry.

4. Glue left middle drawer together in same way.

5. Repeat fit for next partition H.

6. Glue top drawer together.

7. Repeat for second set of three drawers.

8. Top drawers must be free to slide in and out after top is attached. Try for fit, and sand drawer tops down if necessary.

9. Try doors M for fit. Areas on left and right sides of door are cut out to accommodate *your* hinge size. One side of hinge is glued to back of door. Other side of hinge is glued to thin strip of wood which has been glued to inner side of side D. This step will take adjustment and patience. I use instant glue for attaching the hinges, but great

caution must be used to prevent excess glue from getting into the working hinge part.

10. Top piece C is glued into place. Hold in place with weights or rubber bands; allow to dry thoroughly.

11. Several tiny $5/16''$ length strips of wood are cut for drawer and door pulls, and glued into place.

Note: This dresser may be varied by eliminating the right side and just having a six-drawer unit. Another alternative is to complete the right side with drawers, making a wide nine-drawer unit.

## BEDSIDE TABLE

The beauty of this piece, like the dresser, is in the continuous wood grain on the drawers. To be perfectly matched, the drawers must be cut out of one piece of wood.

### Materials
Hardwood (cherry, walnut) $1/16''$, $1/8''$.

### Directions
1. Glue extended bottom piece D to base piece C. Secure tightly with masking tape or clamps, and allow to dry.

2. Try false partition E for bottom position holding sides A and back B in place. Glue E into position on top of D.

3. Glue sides A and back B into position.

4. Construct bottom drawer first. Glue side pieces H and back piece I to bottom piece J. Let dry.

5. Glue front piece G to above structure. Top of drawer should be level. Bottom front will extend $1/16''$ below. Let dry.

6. Put drawer in place. Try partition E for fit above drawer. This should be snug, but still allow drawer to fall out easily. When satisfied, remove drawer and glue partition E into place.

7. Glue top drawer together same as above, adjusting and sanding where necessary.

8. Glue top piece (F) into place.

## TABLE-DESK WITH INLAID TOP

### Maerials
Basswood $1/64''$ (or $1/32''$), $1/8''$; thin leather or leatherette; $1/4''$ square brass tube; $1/4''$ brass strip; paper clip for pegs.

### Directions
1. Glue edge pieces C and D on top of table top piece A. Sand smooth.

2. Try leatherette within center area of A. If edge pieces are too high, sand down so entire surface of wood and leatherette is even and smooth.

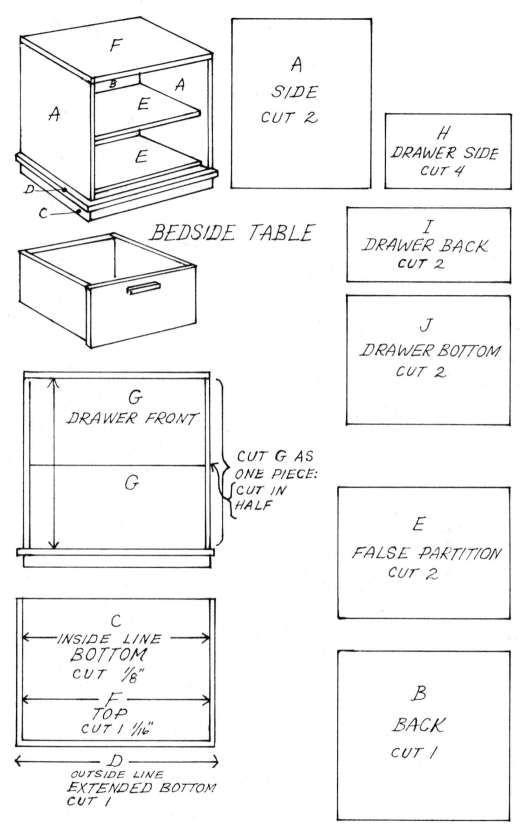

Fig. 7–20 Pattern and assembly guide for bedside table.

Fig. 7–21 Square brass tubing becomes legs for table-desk and side chair. Table top is made of wood, inlaid leatherette and brass sheet. The chair is covered with Haitian cotton and features a decorative handle at top.

3. Paint edges of table top, and side areas that will show, using a color of your choice.

4. Apply several coats of decoupage mixture to painted areas.

5. Glue leatherette piece B onto depressed area of table top. Top should be smooth to touch.

6. Insert and glue small sections of square fitted blocks of wood inside top openings of each brass leg as shown in Fig. 7–22. Sand away excess if necessary for smooth flat surface.

7. Drill down about $1/4''$ in center of each block in brass leg. Insert and glue a piece of clipped paper clip. Clip off excess leaving about $1/16''$ of clip protruding, which will be inserted into underside of table when gluing later. Set aside for now.

8. Glue each piece of brass strip G and H onto respective matching wooden piece E and F. Dry thoroughly.

9. Glue brass legs and strip pieces E-G and F-H into place following Fig. 7–22 for placement. Be sure legs are straight when gluing into place.

*Note:* Top area of table-desk does not have to be painted. Attractive woods can be stained and waxed and leather inlaid area can be another contrasting wood, or create other inlaid designs of wood.

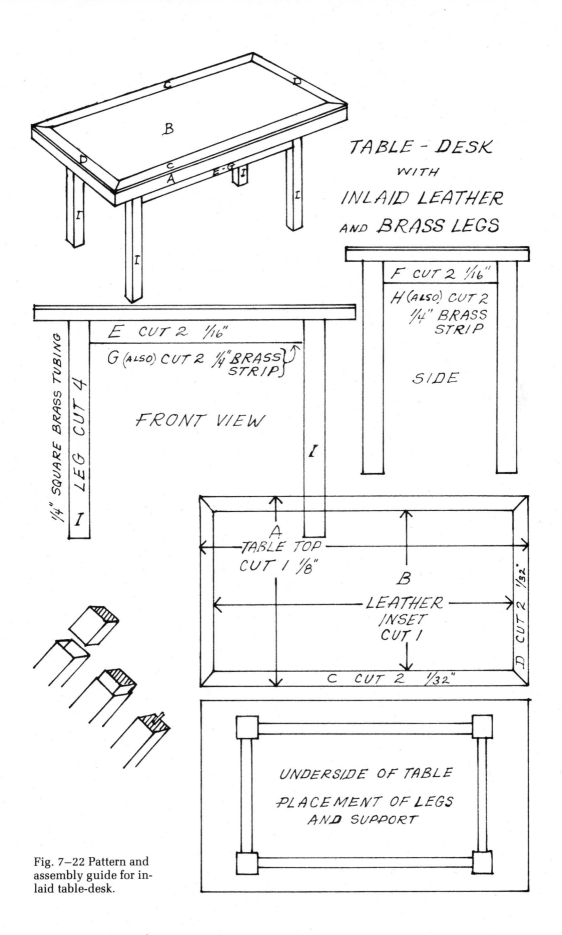

TABLE - DESK
WITH
INLAID LEATHER
AND BRASS LEGS

F CUT 2 ¹⁄₁₆"

H (ALSO) CUT 2 ¼" BRASS STRIP

SIDE

E CUT 2 ¹⁄₁₆"

G (ALSO) CUT 2 ¼" BRASS STRIP

FRONT VIEW

¼" SQUARE BRASS TUBING

LEG CUT 4

I

A
TABLE TOP
CUT 1 ¹⁄₈"

B
LEATHER
INSET
CUT 1

C CUT 2 ¹⁄₃₂"

D CUT 2 ¹⁄₃₂"

UNDERSIDE OF TABLE

PLACEMENT OF LEGS
AND SUPPORT

Fig. 7–22 Pattern and
assembly guide for in-
laid table-desk.

## SIDE CHAIR

### *Materials*

Basswood ¹/₈″; 3-ply bristol board; ³/₁₆″ square brass tube; upholstery material; art foam.

### *Directions*

1. Following dotted lines around pattern piece A, cut out fabric for seat base upholstery. Glue fabric onto seat base A, pulling fabric down and under the four sides.

2. Glue two front legs into position as shown in Fig. 7–23. Allow to dry for several hours.

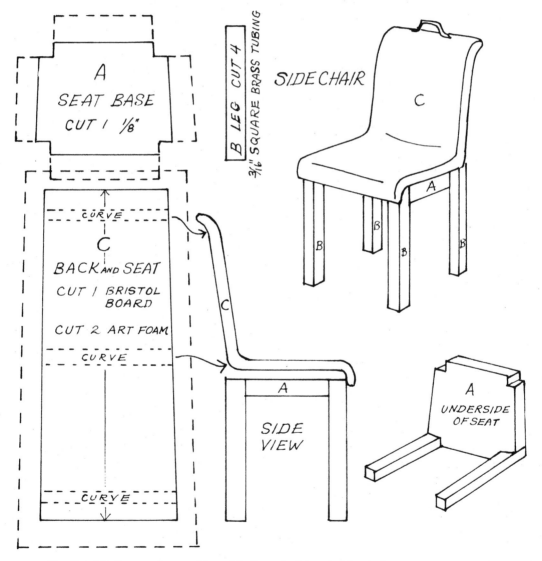

Fig. 7–23 Pattern and assembly guide for upholstered side chair.

3. Curve bristol board in designated areas as shown in Fig. 7–23. Spot-glue two thicknesses of art foam to top side of bristol board. Cover top of art foam with material (indicated by dotted lines). It is spot-glued onto the foam, and the edges are pulled around and glued onto back of board. Trim corners where bulky. Cut material to pattern C and glue to back of seat form. Trim closer if necessary to provide nice finished edging.

4. When front two legs are completely dried, glue back pair of legs into position. Dry several hours.

5. Securely glue seat of C to base piece A, being sure to cover over all four corners. If desired, stuff the corner tube holes with blocks of wood before covering.

## BEDROOM ACCESSORIES

### Three-Way Mirror
The success of this project depends upon the accuracy of the mirror cuts.

#### *Materials*
Mirror; Northeastern frame molding (PFA-4); 4 mini-hinges.

### *Directions*
1. Stain molding to match dresser.

2. Construct frames for each of the three mirrors and glue mirror into frame,

3. Carefully mark off with pencil where hinges should be placed. Glue hinges onto sides of each frame as shown in Fig. 7–25. Be careful that glue does not get into movable part of hinge.

4. Stand mirrors on dresser or mount on wall.

Fig. 7–24 A molded seat and back, a covered base piece and four brass tube legs will become a contemporary side chair.

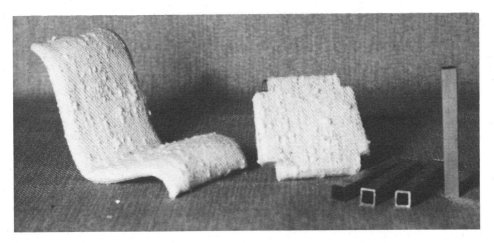

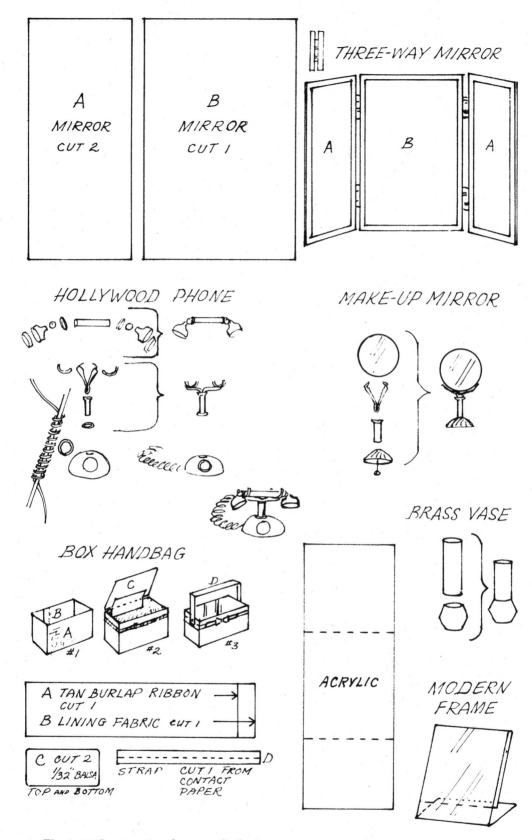

Fig. 7–25 Construction drawings for bedroom accessories.

**Hollywood Telephone**

This project makes up beautifully with the use of metal and jewelry findings and other small items. See Fig. 1–25 for directions and placement.

### Materials

Modeling compound; jewelry findings (links, bail, eyelets); white florist's wire; 3/16" dowel. Use instant glue and all-purpose cement.

### Directions

1. *Base:* The base of the phone is shaped from modeling compound. Round link and eyelet are pressed into clay while still soft and then removed. Allow base to harden.

2. Base is painted a color of your choice. Area within link is painted white. Eyelet and gold link are glued into place.

3. Numbers are delicately added to white circle area. If a photo of dial part can be obtained small enough, so much the better.

4. Bail is spread open; with pliers pinch small extension on bottom together, and glue atop and into eyelet hole. Let dry. Apply cement to each end of bail where prongs turn upward and set half-cut links into each end to hold receiver.

5. *Receiver:* The receiver is glued together in sections allowing glue to dry before next gluing procedure. First paint center (toothpick) section and two small cuttings of 1/4" dowel. When dry, dowel pieces are each glued into a grommet; small gold beads are glued to tiny jump links. Jump links are glued to the tapered ends of toothpick. Grommets are glued to small beads; slant "earphones" and "mouthpiece" slightly inward.

6. *Coiled Line:* Paint or coat six inches of white florist's wire with matching base color mixed with white glue. This will prevent the fiber

Fig. 7–26 Hollywood telephone compared to a thimble.

from unraveling from wire. Let dry. Wrap florist's wire closely around 18-gauge wire. Slip off. Glue one end of coiled line to back of base, and let dry. Work with wire and shape so that other end will be near where you *think* receiver will be. Clip if necessary. This step must be done before receiver is in cradle to prevent breaking the delicate parts. When satisfied with coil arrangement, slip receiver into cradle and glue end of coil near end of receiver.

### Makeup Mirror

#### *Materials*
Round mirror ½"; bail ¼"; eyelet ¼"; finding for base; craft pin.

### *Directions*
1. Bail is spread apart and glued to edge of mirror.
2. Pinch together tip of bail to fit down into eyelet. Glue in place.
3. Craft pin is clipped shorter. Using glue, attach three bottom pieces together.

### Box Handbag

#### *Materials*
Tan burlap ribbon; balsa wood ¹/₃₂"; small print of cotton fabric; contact paper; two sequin pins.

### *Directions*
1. Glue fabric B to wrong side of burlap A. Part of fabric will overlap at the end.
2. Measure and glue burlap-ribbon strip into a box shape. Ends meet at center back. Use the extra fabric as overlap. (See drawing #1 in Fig. 7–25.)
3. Seal balsa top and bottom with stain.
4. Dip bottom edges of burlap-ribbon box into mound of Velverette glue and adhere to bottom piece C. Let dry. Trim edges if necessary.
5. Add ¹/₁₆" cutting of same fabric print around outside of box. (See drawing #2.)
6. Attach cover to box top at rear by gluing small piece of fabric to inside of box and inside of cover. (See drawing #2.)
7. For handle, use anything flexible but strong. I used contact paper, doubled over and stained to match top.
8. Slide pins through handle and box (See drawing #3). Clip pins inside. Apply strong cement adhesive to ends of clipped pins to secure in place.
9. Add petite design or initials to top of cover.

### Brass Vase
Two pieces combine to form a brass vase. Brass tubing (¼") is cut and glued within a brass compression sleeve ¼" O.D. tube. The latter

is purchased in the plumbing section of hardware departments. Fill bottom with some hardening compound to keep flowers or whatever from slipping through.

### Table Frame

Thin acrylic $1/32''$ is folded on dotted lines to form the shape that is shown in Fig. 7–25.

Place a flame tamer on top of a heating element. Apply medium to low heat. When heat seems sufficient, hold acrylic over flame tamer. Heat will begin to soften acrylic. Remove acrylic. Using a flat needle file, quickly fold the acrylic back as drawing shows. Repeat heating for other fold if necessary. It must be worked rather quickly and may take a bit of practice.

Cut a portrait to size (made from a contact print) and slip into frame.

# 8

# Basket Stall

BASKETRY was old in biblical times, yet the art of basket weaving is still as new as any contemporary product today. Lightweight, decorative and useful, baskets have become the catch-all for contemporary storage. They come with and without lids, and in assorted colors, shapes and sizes. They may be simple or extravagantly decorated.

Large ones are used as hampers. Medium-size ones can hold magazines, plants and picnic foods, or serve as waste baskets. Turned upside down, they become lampshades. Small ones provide space for stationery, dried flowers, bathroom items, kitchen tools, and office supplies. And some baskets don't do anything except decorate a wall or hang in groups from the ceiling.

I'm no great hand at basket weaving, which is a slow and meticulous art. The best I can do is simulate some basketry and incorporate them and some purchased baskets into a shop of their own. The shop is only my excuse for encouraging you to use some baskets in your contemporary room settings.

At first I was going to lodge my accumulated baskets in the conventional store-box room, but rummaging around in the basement produced this stall-like construction, gathering dust. This well-built bird house toy structure was made by my husband many years ago.

The original stall box was painted dark green, much too severe for my purpose, and the overhanging roof seemed too large. I cut the roof back one inch, and used a vinyl covering on the interior. Basket designs were painted on the outside walls to attract customers, and the roof was covered with shingles cut from balsa wood. It reminds me of a flea market or boutique shed. Our imaginary owner could simply dismantle everything for storage and return again the next weekend.

Fig. 8–1 The Basket Stall, resurrected from an old toy, is embellished with a wide assortment of baskets, ranging from very tiny to very large. Most of the baskets were purchased; others were fashioned by the author; and the braided baskets and clothespin doll were made by Anneruth Pfister.

## MAKING A STALL

This is a rather heavy piece, with thick wood. Use a thinner wood if desired.

### Directions

1. Glue side pieces D to bottom piece A.
2. Glue back piece B to edges of D and A.
3. Glue the roof structure C to top of D.
4. Add small strips of wood to peak of roof to finish.
5. Glue strip of wood E to fit across front of bottom A.
6. Add a small platform (1¼″ wide) on top of E. Use dowel supports.
7. Paint surface, or decorate as you choose.
8. Add small shelf inside if desired.

## BRAIDED BASKETS

Anneruth Pfister began braiding baskets when she accidentally locked herself out of her home on a bright autumn afternoon. Waiting

Fig. 8–2 An old bird feeder makes an ideal roadside stand or flea market stall.

Fig. 8–3 Fresh paint, vinyl designs, roofing, placemat flooring, and burlap ribbon turn the feeder into a respectable stall ready for merchandise.

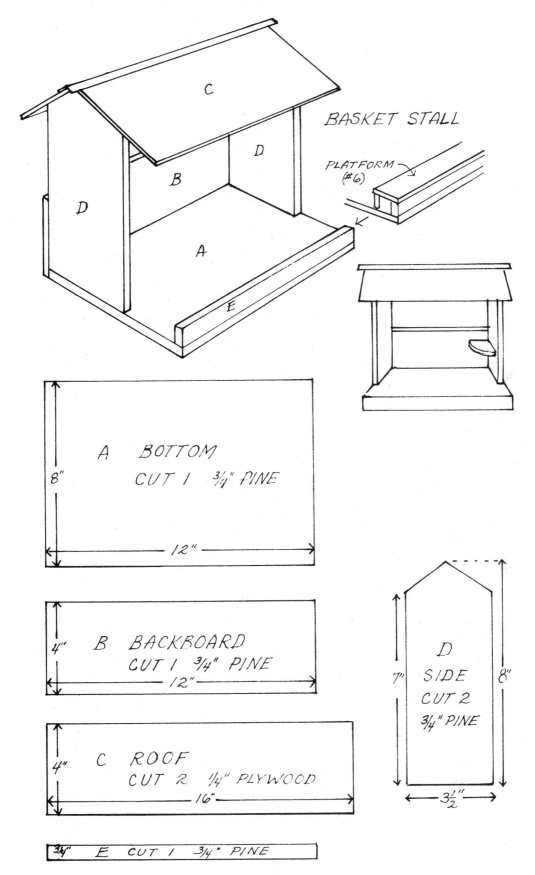

BASKET STALL

PLATFORM (#6)

A    BOTTOM
CUT 1   3/4" PINE

8"

12"

B   BACKBOARD
CUT 1  3/4" PINE

4"

12"

C   ROOF
CUT 2  1/4" PLYWOOD

4"

16"

D
SIDE
CUT 2
3/4" PINE

7"

8"

3 1/2"

3/4"    E  CUT 1   3/4" PINE

Fig. 8—4 Pattern and guide for making a stall.

Fig. 8–5 Anneruth Pfister invented a unique method for creating assorted baskets, cradles, mats and hats by braiding the leaves from dried day lilies.

for her husband's return, she passed the time braiding some dried day lily leaves. A new type of basket was born in the process. Anneruth uses this method for making baskets, cradles, tote bags, mats and hats.

The leaves must have been exposed to a frost and have wilted. The dried leaves are moistened with water; each leaf is gently pulled taut. Anneruth uses the standard three-strand braid, and as one leaf ends,

Fig. 8–6 A finished coiled basket and cover, made from fiber used for weaving.

Fig. 8–7 Coiled basket can be made using bottle caps for form. This particular fiber had fine threads held together with a delicate white shiny thread, providing a woven look.

another is fed into the braid. Any ends that protrude can be cut away with cuticle scissors.

The coil method of basketry is employed, with the coils held together with tan colored thread. Baskets may be sewn with a needle, or made with a wrapping stitch found in any basketry book. Round

Fig. 8–8 Baskets of different shapes and sizes are made from double-mesh Penelope canvas. The mesh is moistened with water and forced around assorted bottle caps and other shapes, securely held with another top until dry.

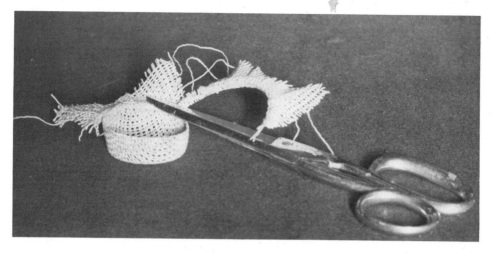

Fig. 8–9 After thorough drying, excess mesh is cut away with scissors.

and oval baskets and tote bags only differ with how each starts the coil. A little braided handle can be sewed on top.

Hats start with a coil shaped over a large bead, and then fanned out. Cradles also start with a coiled-shape base. The hood is started about one-third forward, arched over to the other side and rotated back and forth, curving inward until finished. Small rockers can be cut out of balsa.

## COILED BASKET WITH COVER

Coiled baskets are very easy to make, but the finished effect can be influenced by the selection of twine. Visit a craft store that sells an assortment of products for weaving.

Fig. 8–10 An assortment of simulated baskets.

Bottle caps from mouthwash bottles make ideal forms for coiling purposes. See Fig. 8–7. Waxed paper or plastic wrap should be placed around bottle cap, to keep coils from sticking to cap. Coils are carefully glued together. When finished, if the paper doesn't pull away, line both basket and cover with a pretty cotton print.

## SIMULATED BASKETS

### *Directions*

1. Wet a cut section of tan-colored Penelope 18 doublemesh needlepoint canvas. Push wet mesh evenly around a bottle cap or other suitable unit. Force a second cap over mesh to secure. Allow to dry thoroughly overnight.

2. When dry, excess mesh is cut away with sharp scissors. Make sure edges are perfectly even. With white glue, carefully glue a single strand from mesh around edge of basket to finish.

An assortment of styles, sizes and shapes are shown in Fig. 8–10. Handles can be added by braiding three strands together. Different units can be sewed together to form covers, or tops can be made to slip over bottom sections.

# 9

# Garden Breakfast Room

THIS is a room that I don't have and can never hope to have in real life. But it's not all fantasy. The rattan furnishings are copies of my own table and chairs, and the hand-painted mural of hanging planters is a reasonable facsimile of my kitchen wall mural.

## BOX CONSTRUCTION

This box room is somewhat smaller than I usually make. Lack of space is catching up with me. The box is 16″ wide, 13″ deep and 12″ high. Advantageously, it will fit behind any commercial size frame (12″ × 16″) for front coverage.

There is an extra inner wall with cut-out window and doorway, which is placed approximately 3″ forward of back outer wall. The window on left side wall is cut out matching the size and height of the back window. The cut-out window size in my room is 4″ wide 5¼″ high but you can alter it to suit your tastes.

The size and height of the inner back wall will depend on what you put on the floor. A paper floor takes up no room, but tiles or brick use more space. Some adjustment will be necessary. *Therefore watch the height of the two windows from floor. Be sure they match before cutting the openings.*

The shell of the box is not adhered together until all wall coverings are in place, windows and trim are finished and mural is completed on right wall. Back entrance way and outdoor area must also be finished before assembly.

### Wall Preparation

Cut acrylic to fit two windows; set aside.

Cover left wall and back inner with paper or fabric of your choice.

Cut, measure and miter moldings for windows and doorway.

Fig. 9–1 Lemon yellow and white are the dominant colors of the Garden Breakfast Room. The floor is white ceramic tile with yellow grouting and the wall fabric covering of yellow patterned flowers resembles Oriental silk. The ceiling fan with ping-pong ball "light" is centered over "rattan" furnishings upholstered in Haitian cotton. Paintings are by the author and, the wall-hung weaving peeking through back doorway was made by Marilyn Diesu.

Allow moldings to extend over windows by ⅛″ all around. Acrylic will be inserted later.

Use gesso as primer for moldings; and when dry, paint with color of your choice. Glue painted moldings into place.

Paint half of back outer wall (hall area) on right side with undercoat of gesso, and molding color. Paint back 3″ of right wall to match rear wall hallway.

## Mural

I have a large planter mural on my kitchen wall, and I have received many compliments on it. When planning this room, I thought, if the wall looks so good in people-size, why not in miniature? Although it is intended for a garden breakfast room, this mural would be appealing in any room of a home, shop or restaurant. You can add or deduct to fill the available space, or copy your own favorite plant from a plant book.

Plastic brick pattern from Holgate and Reynolds is glued to wall around the mural. For this room it is painted white, but the color can be adapted to other color schemes.

For the finishing touch picture frame molding from Northeastern Scale Models is painted yellow and glued around the mural. In this case the molding is turned outward, catching onto the rim of the brick edging.

### Windows

Glue acrylic into window openings.

The upper portions of the windows feature facsimile stained glass, which was taken from the book *Ready-to-Use Doll House Stained Glass Windows for Hand Coloring* by Ed Sibbett, Jr. The designs are colored with watercolors.

The stained glass is carefully cut to fit upper area, and with tiny amounts of white glue along edges, is attached to *outside* of acrylic. A thin piece of acrylic is cut to cover the design and is carefully glued over it. If you're careful, glass can be used for windows instead of acrylic. But since *I* smashed one window and cracked the second, *my* preference is acrylic.

Fig. 9–2 The basic cut-outs and eventual assemblage of walls for Garden Breakfast Room.

Fig. 9–3 The right side of the Breakfast Room is diversified with a wall mural of hand-painted plants, hand-made plants, dried plants and even tiny real ones. The yellow decoupaged console table sits against a wall which is embossed with a plastic brick pattern from Holgate and Reynolds.

Fig. 9–4 Plants abound in an embossed brick planter box that wraps around the left side and rear wall of the Breakfast Room. The free-form batik on the side wall was made by Bede Pollets, and the macrame hanging tables in corner by Marilyn Diesu. A handmade dieffenbachia plant is "rooted" in a ceramic pot and a plastic Oriental figure stands in the corner as an art object.

Fig. 9–5 The shade on the window is a cut-out portion of tan casement material, which resembles weaving or macrame. The simulated stain glass top is taken from the book, *Ready-to-Use Doll House Stained Glass Windows for Hand Coloring* by Ed Sibbett, Jr.

Flat muntins about ¼″ wide are cut to fit across both inside and outside of windows to separate the stained area from the clear area.

Very thin strips of wood are glued to the outside of the acrylic and wall area to secure window in place. Molding is added now or later to finish off window.

A fabric table yielded some interesting casement fabric. Cut "just so," it made decorative woven shades which were attached to a box-like structure, and then glued onto the muntins.

**Floor**

For a flooring that is easy to live with and easy to clean, ceramic tile is ideal. An unglazed peppered white selection provided the best background for this room.

The ⁷/₈″ square blocks of tile (held together as a large block) are positioned very easily on the wooden floor of the box. On the left side the tiles required cutting to fit the space. I went back to the store where the owner graciously cut the tiles with a special diamond cutting saw. There's an advantage to doing business with the independent small dealer.

The tile is attached with floor tile adhesive, using directions on the can. The board usually starts to warp quickly. After several minutes, when tile starts to "grab hold," turn floor over, and *thoroughly wet* the wooden surface. Press down (tiles face down) with weights and allow wood to dry at least 24 hours.

After thorough drying, the tiles are grouted using directions on the package. Instead of the usual white, I decided to color the grouting cement a yellow tint to match the color scheme. You can use food coloring or a water-based acrylic paint. I prefer the paint, since there is much greater selection of color.

**The Back Area**

The back area with an approximate depth of 3″ is divided into two sections. The left side represents an outdoor scene with a pathway heading to a door that enters into a small hallway on the right. See Fig. 9–6. The scene on the left is very simply done, with painted blue sky, leafless trees and ground coloring. Lychen, model railroad greenery, is glued on wall to become a hedge along the walkway. The entrance door is painted cream color, as is the house clapboard siding. The "inside" door and wall are painted bright yellow to match the door shutters and molding trim.

Because the "outside area" will be darkened by the top covering, an electrical system should be supplied. A seven-watt bulb and socket are attached to the inside wall and wired out the side; a dimmer system allows the light to switch from bright sunlight to dusk. As seen in Fig. 9–7, a small portion of back wall is cut out (to be able to replace the bulb); it will be hinged back into place after the top is permanently attached.

The walls are finished, and it's time to put them together permanently. Using a strong adhesive, glue left side and outer back wall together and against bottom section. Glue inner wall, and then right side wall into place. Use clamps or tape to hold corners together until dry. Hammer small nails (¹/₂ 20 GA) into joined areas, keeping them evenly spaced.

Fig. 9–6 Back wall of Garden Breakfast Room shows outside–inside entrance hall. Simulated door is in the middle section. The left side is a simple landscape painted with acrylic. The shubbery along "tiled" walk is lychen, a product used in model railroad landscaping.

## Planter Box

A garden room needs planter boxes along window walls. This one is angled at the corner (see Fig. 9–8) allowing for more lush planting and an aesthetic art piece in the corner. The box is 1½" deep and 2" high. The same molded brick pattern used on the right wall covers the outside of the boxes. Fitted and mitered basswood strips are used as capping stones. The brick and wood are painted white. Three separate inside containers are made out of matboard; and the planter is glued snugly against the wall.

A pair of purchased louvered doors are painted yellow and attached to the sides of the inside doorway. The ceiling is covered with commercial white ceiling paper, and the ceiling paddle fan, previously made, is glued to the ceiling.

Furnishings and other accessories are placed into position.

The box can be protected from dust with a framed acrylic front, attached with side hinges. Extra blocks of wood have been glued to the underside of box to allow for frame width.

Fig. 9–7 After ceramic tile floor and individual wall units are finished off, the structure is put together with strong adhesive and tiny nails. Electrification with a 7-watt bulb in left rear section provides "daylight effect" from bright to dusk with a dimmer attachment. Brick flower section has three inserts made from matboard. Rear cut-out section will be hinged to permit bulb replacement and air circulation.

## RATTAN TABLE

### Materials
³/₁₆″ dowel sticks (2); brown or dark tan extra-strong button and carpet thread; 5″ diameter stainless steel bowl (or whatever) for bending dowels.

### Directions
1. Cut dowel sticks into 5″ lengths and soak in boiling water.

2. Bend dowels around a round object of 5″ diameter, as shown in Fig. 9–10. Secure with masking tape or rubber bands. Dry overnight.

3. Using Fig. 9–12 as guide, cut four curved dowels to match legs of table piece A, as shown in Fig. 9–11.

4. Stain all pieces the same color selected for chairs. Birch or walnut is suggested.

5. Incise both ends of all B pieces for good fit. See drawing in Fig. 9–12. Use pencil marks to keep them matched.

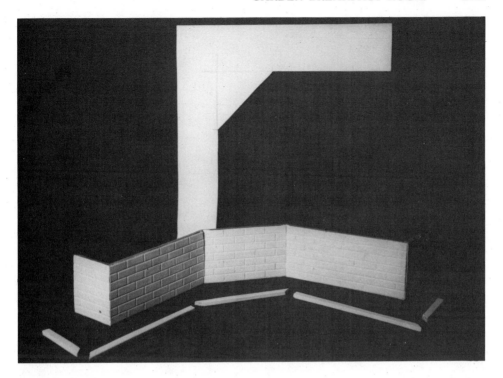

Fig. 9–8 Cut-out form on top is pattern used to form structure of planter shape. Planter was formed from illustration board and covered with embossed plastic brick. Basswood "cap stones" are in front of planter.

Fig. 9–9 Rattan furniture reproduced in miniature. Twine trim (button thread) and Haitian cotton upholstery provide a finished look. Round glass tabletop was cut by a professional glass cutter. Small gold beads become "rolling casters" on chair-leg bottoms.

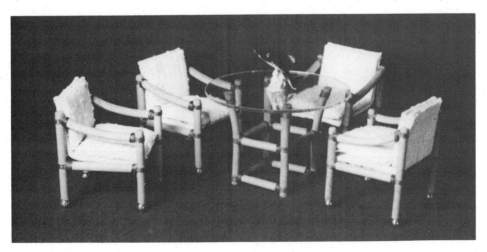

Fig. 9–10 Water-soaked dowels are forced around a steel bowl. Strong rubber bands hold dowels in place until dry.

6. Using Fig. 9–12 as a guide, glue and wrap button thread on leg pieces A. Wrappings on B pieces should be done after gluing pieces together. Use 6″ lengths of thread for windings.

7. Before gluing bottom pieces B to lower part of pieces A do realize that the upper curved part of A turns outward at a 45° angle. *Do not lay the pieces flat on the drawing to glue.* Proceed to glue lower part of table and allow to set well. Glue upper pieces B to upper legs of table. Dry well.

8. Place a 3½″ round of glass or acrylic atop legs. Use a tiny amount of instant bonding adhesive to keep glass from slipping. Glass should be purchased from a dealer who can cut it to the size needed.

## RATTAN ARMCHAIR

### *Materials*
³/₁₆″ dowels; ⅛″ strips of wood; brown or tan extra strong button and carpet thread; birch or walnut stain; Titebond glue or other yellow glue; four gold beads, ³/₁₆″; upholstery fabric.

### *Directions*
For proper alignment use graph paper and wax paper with gluing procedure. Each chair requires eighteen 6″ lengths of button thread for twine wrappings.

1. Soften 6″ piece of dowel in boiling water and bend around 5″ diameter bowl or equivalent. Hold in place with rubber bands. (See Fig. 9–10.) Dry overnight.

2. Round off tops of pieces A and B with sandpaper or file.

3. Stain pieces (A, B, C, D, E and F) with birch or walnut stain.

4. Applying a small circle of glue, wrap button thread around pieces A and B as indicated on Fig. 9–12. Four times around is sufficient. Clip both ends on same side and glue down.

5. Pieces C and D need incising on each end, so they will glue more securely against upright pieces. Mark two small lines with pencil at each end, to help line up *even* incising area. Use needle file for incising.

6. Apply small dabs of glue to areas of twine on A and B and ends of C and D. Allow to become tacky. Press C against twine on A and B. Insert and press D against twine on A and B. Repeat for other side. Add additional *white glue* in crevices. Dry thoroughly.

7. Incise both ends of back piece E.

8. Glue into place between back legs B against twine. Be sure side pieces remain straight. Add extra glue in crevices.

9. Glue two slats F into place across seat area connecting C with C. Let dry.

Fig. 9–11 Curved dowel is placed on drawing (use Fig. 9–12) to determine where cuts should be made.

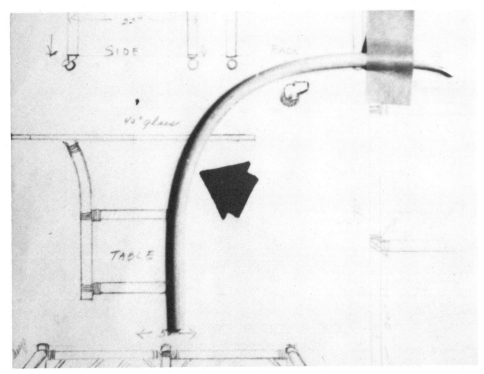

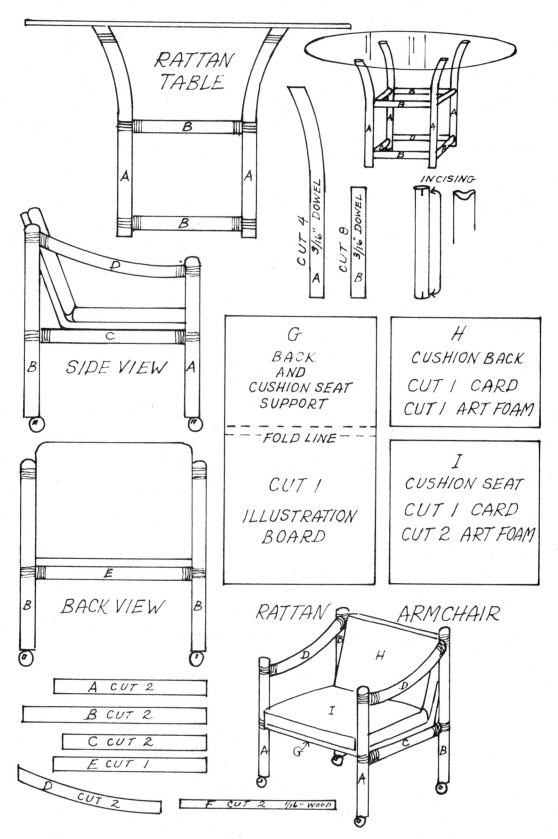

Fig. 9–12 Pattern and assembly guide for rattan table and armchair.

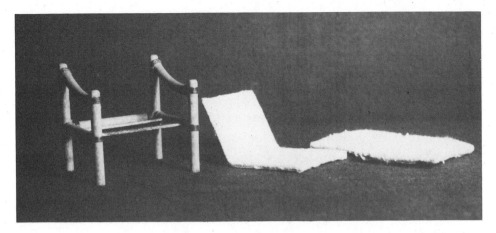

Fig. 9–13 Frame structure of rattan chair is shown before upholstered pieces are attached.

10. Glue and wrap button thread "twine" around rest of arms D, side pieces C and back piece E,

11. Drill hole through bottom center of each leg about ⅛″ deep.

12. Push head pin through gold bead. Clip off excess amount of pin leaving ⅛″ to be inserted into leg. Apply adhesive to leg bottom and insert pin with bead. Repeat for other three legs.

Fig. 9–14 The console table is bright yellow with decoupaged flowers. The dieffenbachia and corn plants are made from hand-painted masking tape. The unique plant holder begins with a lovely ceramic macrame bead as a base. Aluminum tubing is the center post with 18-gauge aluminum wire bent to hold three baskets. Tiny terra cotta flower pots rest on the bead table base.

**Upholstery for Rattan Chair**

1.  Cut fabric for support piece G allowing ¼″ *extra* fabric all around. Using tacky adhesive, glue fabric to board G. Pull and glue extra fabric over to other side. Clip away excess fabric at corners, so fabric lies flat. Cut second piece of fabric the same size as piece G, and glue to back of G.

2.  Spot-glue art foam to card H. Cover cushion back H the same way that G was covered.

3.  Spot-glue two pieces of art foam to card I. Cover cushion seat as above.

4.  Bend support piece G into position to fit within chair and glue into place.

5.  Glue back cushion H and seat cushion I into place.

## DECOUPAGED CONSOLE TABLE

This table is very easy to make, yet is beautiful when finished. The size is 5″ long, but it can be adjusted depending upon personal need.

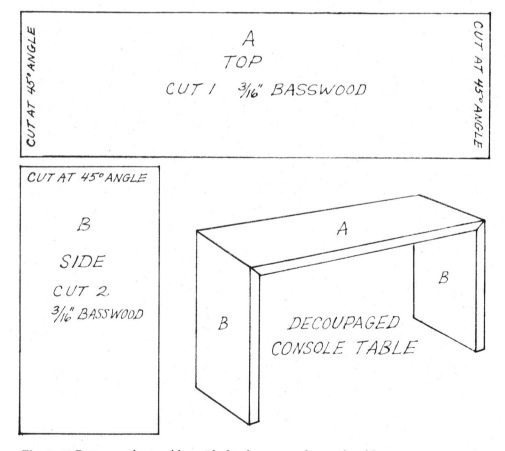

Fig. 9–15 Pattern and assembly guide for decoupaged console table.

### Materials

Basswood sheet ³/₁₆″; small floral paper prints of your selection or whatever print design you may prefer; decoupage finish (Aqua Podge, Mod Podge or clear wood finish such as Deft).

### Directions

1. Carefully cut out prints with cuticle scissors. Work out arrangement. Set prints aside.

2. Sides of top piece A and top of side pieces B are beveled at a 45° angle. Try corner joinings for good fit; sand if necessary.

3. Glue piece A and one piece B together. Let dry and repeat with second piece B.

4. Cut two strips of ¹/₁₆″ wood about 1″ long. Glue on underside, snug into each corner, for extra reinforcement. Let dry completely.

5. Sand table with fine sandpaper; wipe with tack cloth.

6. Apply two even applications of acrylic paint (color of your choice), allowing each coat to dry thoroughly.

7. Lightly sand surface with extra-fine sandpaper. Apply the cut-out prints with diluted glue. Be sure of your placement before gluing. If you wish to add some stems or extra tiny leaves, this can be done with acrylic paint.

8. Apply coat of decoupage finish over print and rest of table; underside too. Allow to dry. Time allowance for drying will vary according to finish you select to use. Follow manufacturer's instructions.

9. Continue to apply more finishings as needed. Sand the surface with extra fine sandpaper after every two brushings. Enough finishing has been applied when surface area of both print and table feel smooth to the touch.

*Note:* If you don't have any decoupaging finish available try using a half-and-half mixture of white (clear) glue and water. Mix well and keep in a covered jar. I have found that several coats will produce a smooth satin finish.

## PLANTS

Miniature plants are made from many materials, from soft fabrics to hardened clay. The goal is to acquire the most realistic look possible. Color of plant, thinness of leaves and drapery of foliage are the priorities. In order to achieve the most accurate colorations, I feel that it's necessary to use paint, which can render the different flecks of color or pattern that distinguish one plant from another. The directions that follow will hopefully help the reader achieve more realism in miniature plant life. Try to obtain color pictures or the plants themselves, so that the leaf color can be duplicated as closely as possible. Note that the underside of a leaf is usually *lighter* in color than the top.

Fig. 9–16 A plastic meat tray makes a useful, disposable palette. Masking tape is placed on waxed paper for painting. Note how paintbrush bristles are splayed for applying paint with dibbling effect.

A foam plastic tray used in supermarkets for meat packing makes a good palette.

### Corn Plants

*Materials*
1″ masking tape; 1/2″ green florist's tape; acrylic paints; 6″ antiseptic swab stick; tacky glue.

*Directions*
1.  Cut piece of wax paper 10″ × 10″ and place on working board. Set out five strips of masking tape, each 8″ long, sticky side down on wax paper. Repeat on *another* sheet. Each sheet is painted a different color.

2.  Mix color to match underside of leaf, and apply to one entire set of masking tape. The color will be a shade of light olive green. Set aside to dry.

3.  Mix slightly darker color to match upper side of leaf, and apply to second set of strips. The upper leaf of a corn plant has a lighter green streak down through the middle, so add a "slim" lighter stroke in a couple of sections of the entire length of each tape where you *think* you will be cutting. Blend streak into leaf color slightly. Dry very well.

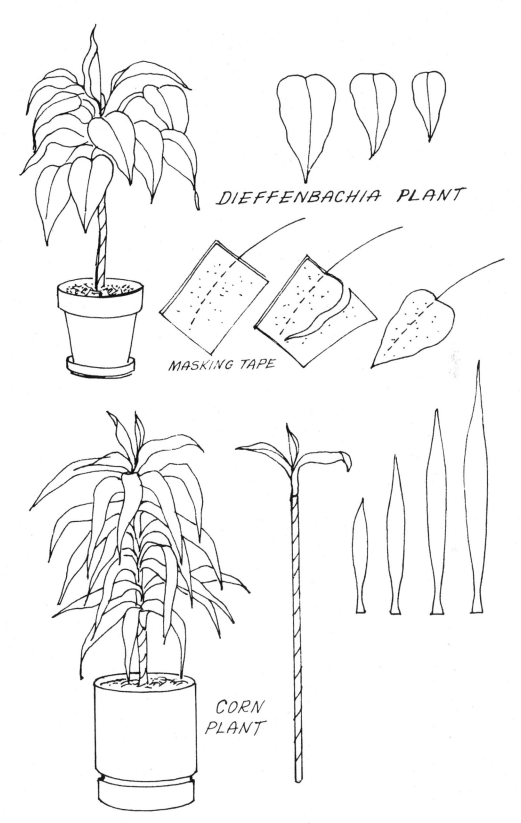

DIEFFENBACHIA PLANT

MASKING TAPE

CORN
PLANT

Fig. 9–17 Pattern and guide for constructing dieffenbachia plant and corn plant.

4. Wrap florist's tape around swab stick for stem.

5. Carefully strip off one tape of each color and stick back to back. Smooth out, and repeat for other four sets of tapes.

6. Using the leaf pattern drawings in Fig. 9–17, cut out as many leaves as you can from the tapes. Cut two or three of the smaller sizes, and the rest should be large. Try to have the lightened area going down through the center. If lightened area seems inadequate, paint a thin, light green line down leaf center and smooth with finger *after* leaves are cut out.

7. Using the blade of a scissors, curl each leaf in an arch, dark side up.

8. To help the leaf cling to the stick fold at the base of each leaf.

9. Starting at the top of stick with the smallest leaves, glue leaves in a continuous downward spiral until plant reaches desired size. Corn plants usually have an area of bare stem, so do not continue leaves to soil level.

10. Set in a "floor" pot of your choice.

## Dieffenbachia

### Materials

1″ wide masking tape; ½″ wide green florist's tape; green florist's wire; acrylic paints; tacky glue.

### Directions

1. Lay down several strips of masking tape on two separate sheets of waxed paper.

2. Apply a light silver-green color to surface of one set of masking tapes for underside of leaf color. Set aside to dry.

3. The top of a dieffenbachia leaf is mottled and variegated. Place in tray three different shades of olive green, a dark green, and some cream color. Swirl some of each of the green colors across the second set of masking tapes creating a marbleized effect. Dip a small brush in the cream color, splay the bristles, and gently dab *very small* cream-colored spots here and there on top of green marbleized effect. With paper toweling gently press down on painted surface to smooth away blobs of paint. Let dry thoroughly.

4. Carefully strip away piece of masking tape of top and bottom colors. Using amount needed for size of leaf to be cut, stick two pieces together with 3″ piece florist's wire set between the tapes. Press down well, accentuating raised effect in center of leaf, as shown in Fig. 9–17.

5. Using leaves in Fig. 9–17 as patterns, cut out leaves with cuticle scissors. Cut out a couple of smaller size, and then large ones.

6. Using darker green paint, accent some of the dark areas on leaf such as the rib down the center and the outside edging of leaf. Add mottled dark areas and drybrush *light* areas where needed. Use your finger to merge colors.

7. Starting at the top with the smallest leaves, wind florist's tape tightly around wires. Continue adding larger size leaves as you proceed downward. Leave approximately ½" of bare wire for leaf stems.

8. Plan for about a 3" plant; but it can be taller or shorter, depending upon your available space. If there is much plant stem to be shown, add tiny cream colored stripe marks to indicate loss of leaves. Two or three plants can be put into one large pot for a very lush effect. Because of the center wiring, the foliage can be easily shaped and draped.

## HANGING PLANTER WALL MURAL

The mural is painted onto illustration board or mat bristol board purchased from art supply store. Water color paints or acrylic paints may be used, with appropriate, very small brushes.

The planters should show a little contour or turning quality, which is accomplished by applying darker values on one side of the planter, and lightening the value as it goes to the other side of pot.

The plants shown in my mural are wandering Jew, impatiens, spider plant, fuchsia, and begonia. You can add or subtract plants according to available space.

The completed mural is cut from the board and is finished off with Northeastern Scale Models frame molding.

Fig. 9–18 Drawing of hanging planter mural.

## CEILING PADDLE FAN

### Materials

Ping pong ball; wood sheet $1/16''$ (cherry, walnut or basswood); gold filigree bead cap with four separations $3/4''$ long; dowel $1/2''$, $3/16''$; two large buttons (shank removed); other brass findings and parts (see Fig. 9–19); multi-purpose craft cement Bond 527 and instant cement; use bits of cotton to help gluing process if necessary.

### Directions

1. Stain or paint wooden paddles, and let dry.
2. Start to glue lower part of construction A. Set ball in an inverted bottle cap to dry.
3. Separate four sections of beadcap with clippers. Cut away small sections of filigree at upper part of each cap leaving center upper section for gluing. With needle nose pliers (filigree facing upward), gently twist each top section only to a slight angle.
4. Glue each bottom tip of filigree section to inner portion of each paddle. Dry well.
5. Try filigree tips for size; they shouldn't overlap. Cut away more filigree if necessary. Using instant glue (I used Permabond Super glue)

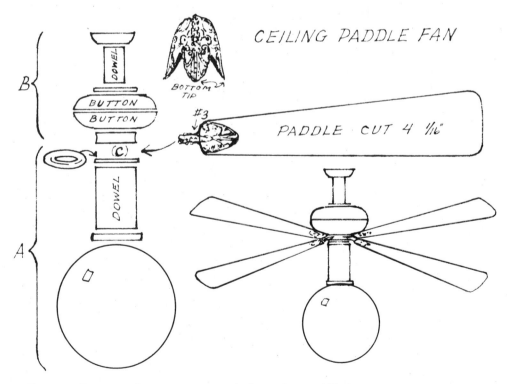

Fig. 9–19 Pattern and construction guide for ceiling paddle fan.

Fig. 9–20 A ping pong ball (light fixture) is balanced within a bottle cap to dry. The rest of the assembled parts are glued piece by piece to simulate a ceiling paddle fan.

fasten each paddle fan into place at C. Hold down filigree securely for several minutes until secure. Allow paddles to dry completely before continuing with construction.

6. Continue gluing rest of construction B.

7. If blades need to be leveled, correct carefully, but all blades should have the same slight slant.

8. Paint all pieces except fan blades and ping pong ball gold.

9. When room is finished and before furnishings are in place, glue structure to ceiling. Pegging will be helpful.

## PLANT HOLDER

This plant holder (see Fig. 9–14) starts with a ceramic macrame bead 2″ high and 1³/₄″ across the top. Clay is forced down through the bead opening, and a 6″ length of aluminum tubing (¹/₈″) is pushed down through the clay. Three pieces of 18-gauge wire are shaped and inserted through top opening of tubing. Baskets of plants are hung on curved ends of wire and small pots sit on bead, which serves as a table top.

# 10

# Record Shop

IF YOU haven't tried doing a shop yet, you're missing a lot of fun. After considering several small businesses, I decided that a Record Shop would surely provide a challenging and exciting venture. My previous shops had all been 20″ wide, and I wondered if I'd be able to fit everything in my new 16″ width dimension. I did sacrifice the check-out counter in lieu of more interesting accoutrements.

## SHOP FIXTURES

It's always a challenge to try to distinguish a room in some small way, so that it doesn't end up with just three walls of shelves and merchandise. Using my favorite device of step-up areas, two back corner arrangements show forbidding black doors leading into office and stock-room space. The doors are made from plywood, sold in model hobby shops, and finished off with plain molding, hinges and doorknobs.

A terrific upholstery fabric remnant with blocks of colors (blue, white, flecks of brown and black) was transformed into carpeting to establish the color scheme. Since this carpet has a rather busy pattern, the identical corner step-up areas were kept simple.

Light brown cork sheeting is applied as the wall covering, and the ceiling is painted bright lemon yellow. Although doors and furnishings are painted black, the accent colors are turquoise and yellow.

A unique ceiling fixture is made from a ping-pong ball (light bulb) glued into a yellow bottle cap which is fitted through the opening of a small record. Displays hang from the edge of the record, with other displays attached to the ceiling. An ambitious miniaturist would have electrified the contraption producing a revolving illuminated fixture, but I never said *I* was ambitious.

The shop is stocked with record albums, tapes, cartridges,

Fig. 10–1 The Record Shop is stocked with record albums and displayed merchandise. Two corner step-up areas lead to doors labeled Office and Stockroom. Standing displays, posters and hanging ceiling displays provide added commercial interest. A real record is used as a novel ceiling fixture. A speaker box is visible above office door.

magazines, posters and various equipment necessary for the record-playing crowd. The speaker box (upper left) and "rip-off" mirror (upper right) are two necessary fixtures. If this room is still around generations from now, will anyone ponder disco dancing, *Star Wars* and Elvis?

## RECORD STAND

### *Materials*

Pinewood or basswood $1/16''$, $1/8''$, $1/4''$; black acrylic paint; Northeastern window sash $3/16''$; three-ply bristol board.

### *Directions*

1. Glue side pieces B to back piece A.
2. Glue base piece C near bottom of pieces A and B.

Fig. 10–2 The basic shop before displays are added. Cork sheeting is applied to walls. Corner platforms and steps are constructed from balsa wood and glued into place after carpeting is down. A mural made from record album stamps (mail advertisement) is added on the back wall. Penelope double mesh canvas, painted black and edged with 18-gauge wire, is used for side walls of platforms. Bottom pieces of wire are forced down into balsa wood and straight sides are glued to wall.

3. Paint entire surface black (or color of your choice).

4. Try sliding pieces F (window sash) for fit. Glue two sections together. See Fig. 10–7 for gluing position. Repeat for upper slide. Paint black the parts that will show, but paint *very lightly* into slotted areas.

5. Add some handles to each outer side of sliding doors G which have been painted color of your choice.

6. Glue first *set* of sliding section F onto front part of base piece C.

7. Fit sliding doors G into slotted section and try upper slotted section for fit. Mark position on ends with pencil. Remove. Apply small dabs of glue at each pencil marked side of B where sliding sections will be glued into position.

8. Slip rear door into *rear* slotted area, top and bottom. Slip front door into *front* slotted area. Be sure they are in their proper slots and sliding back and forth easily. Allow upper slotted pieces F to dry with doors in place.

9. Try upper tray piece D and front face piece E for position. Trim if necessary. When satisfied with fit, glue D and E in place.

Fig. 10–3 The right side of the Record Shop has a peg board filled with the tiniest of essentials, including batteries and wires. Record holders and tape deck holders are made from colored plastic, wood and paper clips. Near the ceiling, the shop has a "rip-off" deterrent mirror which is really a 2″ blind spot mirror purchased in an automotive department.

Fig. 10–4 The left side of the shop displays cassettes, tapes, children's records, magazines and posters. A snappy-looking model from a boutique catalog has a disco album placed in her hand. Posters are arranged on wall.

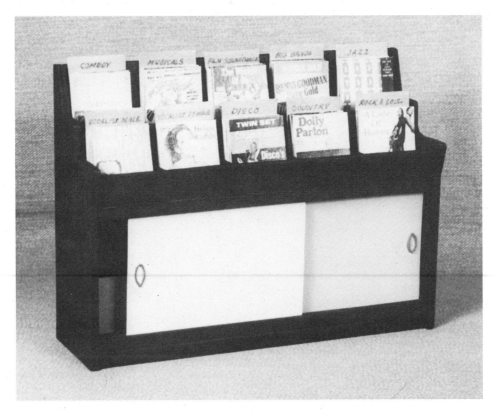

Fig. 10–5 A black record stand with colorful yellow and blue sliding doors holds different selections of "record albums" cut from a Medley catalog. Top section is compartmented and labeled with various styles of music.

10. Using balsa wood, build up three blocks to glue within back trough space to raise upper shelf area about ³/₄". See Fig. 10–6.

11. Glue shelf piece H on top of blocks.

12. Glue upright piece I to piece H and sides B. Slant top of I backward slightly.

13. Division pieces J will need adjustment so cut a top and bottom pattern out of card. Check for fit before cutting all eight pieces of ¹/₁₆" wood. When satisfied with fit, glue dividers into place.

14. Paint black (or your color choice) and touch up previously painted areas where needed.

## TAPE STAND

### *Materials*

Sheets of pine or basswood ¹/₁₆", ¹/₃₂", ³/₈"; acrylic ¹/₃₂"; color prints of stacked tapes—these are photographed in color from advertisements; the size must be small. See Fig. 10–4 and 10–8.

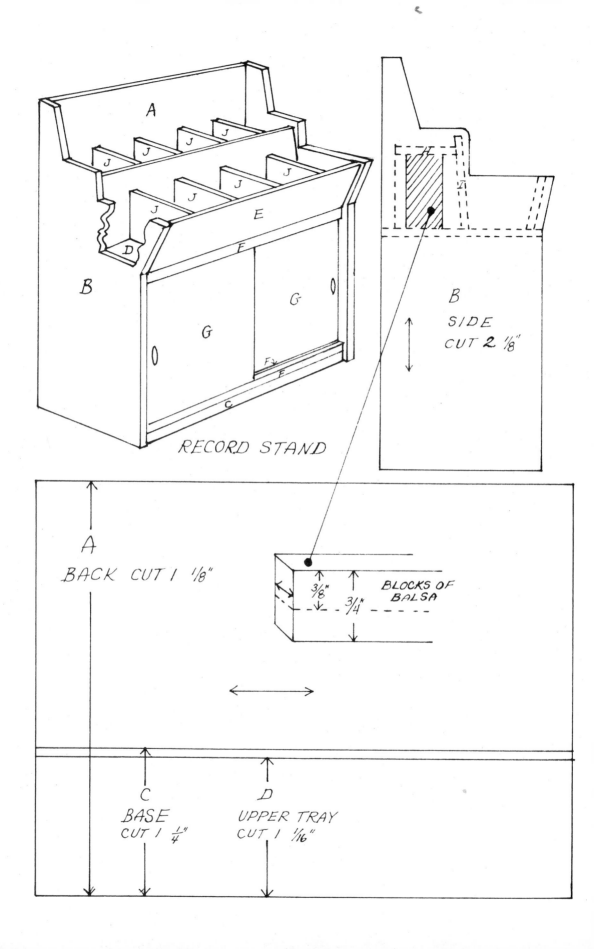

RECORD STAND

A

B

D

E

E

G

G

F

C

J J J J

J J J J

B
SIDE
CUT 2 1/8"

A
BACK CUT 1 1/8"

3/8"

3/4"

BLOCKS OF
BALSA

C
BASE
CUT 1 1/4"

D
UPPER TRAY
CUT 1 1/16"

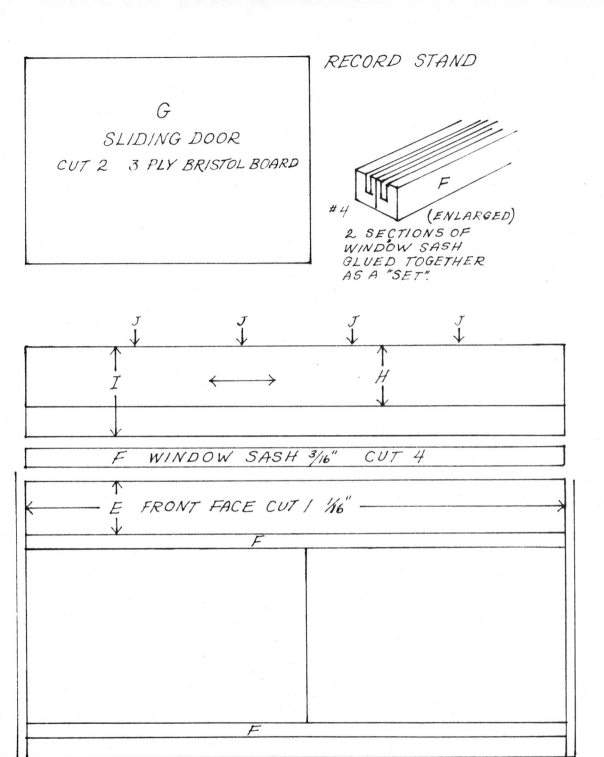

RECORD STAND

G

SLIDING DOOR

CUT 2   3 PLY BRISTOL BOARD

#4

F

(ENLARGED)

2 SECTIONS OF
WINDOW SASH
GLUED TOGETHER
AS A "SET".

J   J   J   J

I       H

F   WINDOW SASH 3/16"   CUT 4

E   FRONT FACE CUT 1 1/16"

F

F

Fig. 10–7 Pattern and assembly guide (continued) for record stand.

Fig. 10–6 Pattern and assembly guide for record stand.

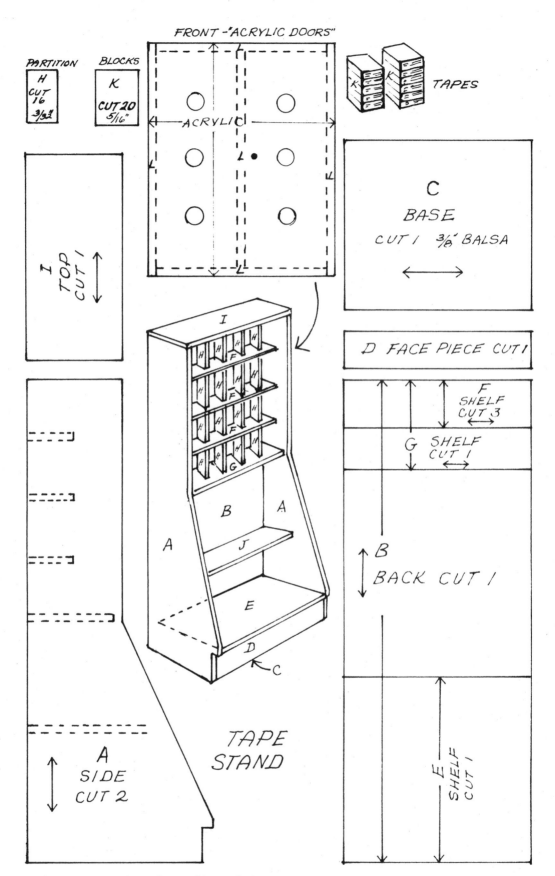

Fig. 10–8 Pattern and assembly guide for tape stand.

Fig. 10–9 The side pieces of the tape stand are taped together before cutting out the pattern, to assure perfect matching pieces.

### *Directions*

1. With pencil, mark off line areas inside of sides A where shelves will be glued. See dotted lines in Fig. 10–8

2. Glue left side piece A to base piece C and back piece B.

3. Repeat with right side piece A.

4. Glue shelf piece E on top of base piece C.

5. Glue face piece D in front of base piece C.

6. Glue shelf pieces F into place.

7. Glue shelf piece G into place.

8. Glue partition pieces H into place on shelves. There are four partition pieces for each shelf, evenly spaced. There will be some adjustments here, so it is better to cut some pieces as you go along.

9. Glue top piece I on top of A's and B.

10. Cut, fit and glue shelf piece J into bottom area.

11. Paint stand black.

### Blocks of Tapes

1. Blocks of wood K are faced with cut-outs of photographed reproductions of *stacks* of tapes; these can usually be found in magazines or catalogs. The blocks are cut to different heights, accommodating a different number of tapes in each grouping.

2. Blocks of tapes are glued into position on upper four shelves between partitions.

### Acrylic "Sliding Doors"

1. With paper punch, cut out six holes in acrylic as indicated on drawing.

2. Cut out ten strips of wood $1/32''$ as indicated by letter L. Paint all strips silver.

3. Glue five strips to surface of acrylic as indicated on Fig. 10–8. Turn over and glue second set of strips on reverse side.

4. Where black dot is, glue a clipped straight pin through acrylic, to represent a lock.

5. Apply glue to appropriate edges of A, I and G. Carefully set entire acrylic front into place.

Make some magazines from advertisements or photograph your own, and stack on the bottom shelves.

## PORTABLE FLOOR STAND

### *Materials*

Latch rug mesh; formica or $1/16''$ wood; four large paper clamps; Testors PLA silver enamel.

### *Directions*

1. Fold mesh on lines as indicated on view A, Fig. 10–11.

2. Apply tacky glue to four edges of square B, along bottom line of mesh (see drawing) catching top of each clip under mesh and along tips of mesh on one side. Press mesh around square. Hold firmly, for several minutes, and let dry.

3. Paint mesh with silver enamel.

*Note:* Instead of using mesh, hardware cloth can be substituted. This is already metal and silver in finish.

## ACCESSORIES

### Cassette Holder

#### *Materials*

Walnut or basswood stained walnut $1/32''$ and $1/16''$; two paper clips $1\,1/4''$ long; four glass rocaille beads; half link for handle; round cut of thick cardboard for bottom.

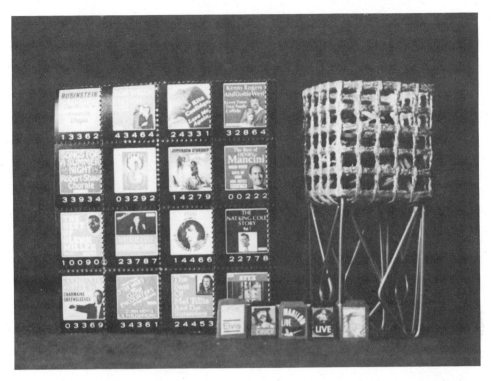

Fig. 10–10 The stand is white mono interlock canvas (four holes per 1″), painted silver and mounted on large paper clip legs. Cassette tapes are small blocks of wood covered with small cutouts from ½″ size advertising stamps.

### Directions

1. Tape two pieces of A together, with grain running in same direction. Drill four small holes through both pieces. (See view #1 on Fig. 10–11.) Mark with pencil one of the sides of both pieces to remember proper alignment.

2. Apply yellow glue to four straight areas on bottom piece A; Glue pieces B into place on bottom piece A. Dry thoroughly.

3. Apply glue to top of pieces B and attach top piece A. Be sure pencil marks previously made match direction.

4. Cut four pieces of paper clip about 1″ long. Put pieces through matching holes on top and bottom; clip off excess. Put a dot of glue on each end.

5. Glue four rocaille beads to cover the clipped off tips on top, and glue handle in center.

6. Glue small round of cardboard to bottom.

### Cartridge Cases

### Directions

Patterns are cut out of thin leatherette or stiff fabric. Flaps are glued in place, forming a case. Top handles are added and a metal doo-dad becomes the front snap.

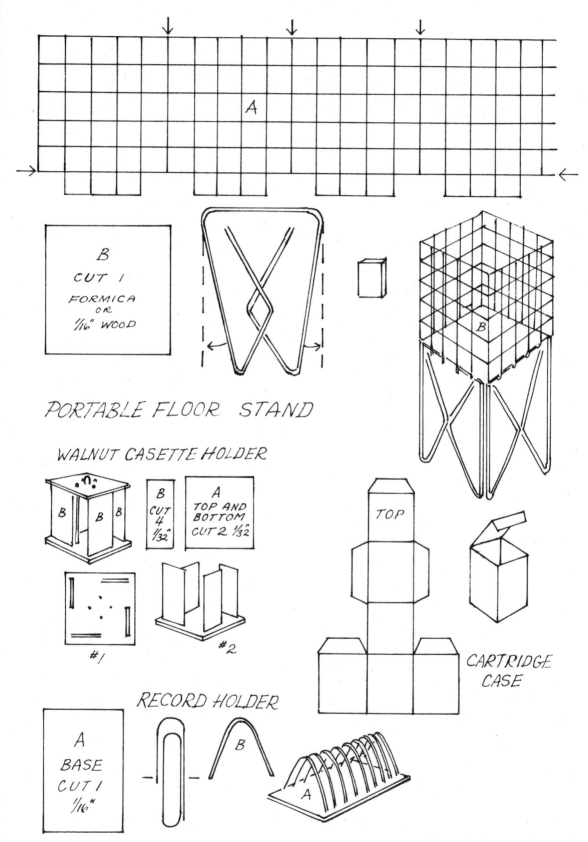

A

B
CUT 1
FORMICA
OR
1/16" WOOD

B

PORTABLE FLOOR STAND

WALNUT CASETTE HOLDER

B    B    B

B
CUT
4
1/32"

A
TOP AND
BOTTOM
CUT 2 1/32"

#1

#2

TOP

CARTRIDGE
CASE

RECORD HOLDER

A
BASE
CUT 1
1/16"

B

A

Fig. 10–11 Pattern and assembly guide for portable floor stand and accessories.

**Record Holder**

### Materials
Basswood ¹/₁₆″; 9 paper clips 1¹/₄″ long.

### Directions
1. Mark off pencil dots (¹/₈″ apart) on two sides of base piece A. Drill holes at each dot, slanting outward. Paint the base piece as desired.
2. Cut paper clips at arrows, and bend outward slightly.
3. Apply thick tacky glue along holes, and brush away excess with finger. Using needle nose pliers, insert one piece B into each set of holes.

**Records**

### Directions
Cut a 1″ round piece of thin cardboard. Pierce centers for hole. Paint both sides black; let dry. Apply white glue over paint for glazed effect. Add small white round piece with color design in center.

**Poster Carton**
Although often unrelated, posters seem to be a part of record departments, and subjects include everything from kittens to noted musical celebrities.

Fig. 10–12 The speaker box is walnut wood, with a nylon hosiery front. The tape stand is basswood. An acrylic front with round punched holes protects the tapes. A simple platform block stand of two levels holds piles of record albums. Advertisement from catalog is glued onto handmade carton holding rolled up posters. A carton holds more record albums.

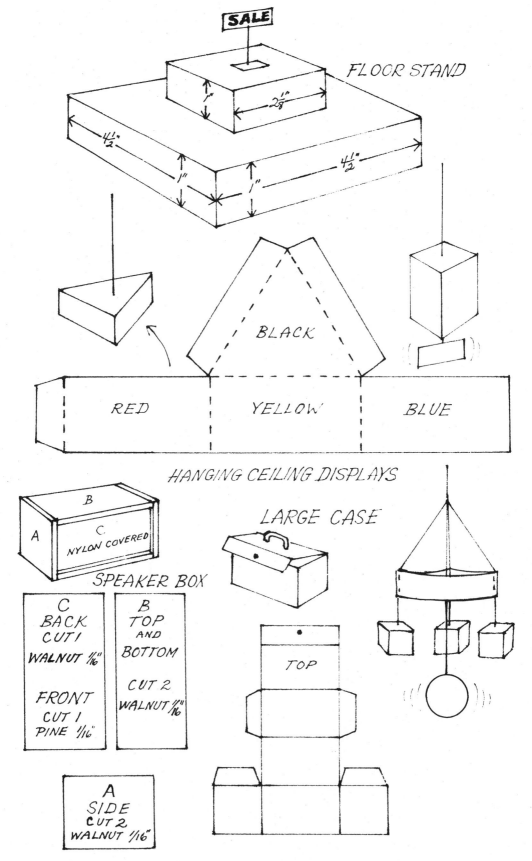

Fig. 10–13 Instruction and assembly guide for Record Shop accessories.

The carton is made by carefully stripping away the outer covering on a corrugated box. This is a good tough brown paper. There will be noticeable parallel ridges left by the corrugated part, which make the paper very easy to fold. Decide your own size of paper before cutting. This one is approximately 3¹/₄″ high, 1³/₄″ wide and ⁷/₈″ deep to accommodate some super photos of "Charlie's Angels."

### Floor Stand

This is essentially a layered floor piece which is usually placed near the entrance door. It's covered with records that are featured specials and reduced in price. Perfectly square in shape (4¹/₄″ × 4¹/₄″ lower level) the reader is left on his/her own to work this one out.

### Hanging Display

An advertising hanging display adds a bit of showmanship to the store. Fold on the dotted lines and glue in the flaps. Size may be adjusted to fit available advertising material. Add a string through the top to hang.

### Speaker Box

Cover surface of pine piece C with a cutting from discarded nylon stocking. Pull nylon around to back and glue.

Glue pieces of A, B, C together. Front piece is recessed a tiny bit. Polish wood surface.

### Long Cartridge Case

Cut the pattern out of leatherette; fold and glue together. Add a handle and a small metal "snap button" on front.

# 11

# One-Room Efficiency Apartment

THIS apartment is a scrap room. It costs very little to construct because it's made up of throw-away junk, unused items around the house, products left over from other miniature jobs and available necessities such as wood. This one-room efficiency apartment cost less than ten dollars (lighting fixture excluded).

## MAKING AND FINISHING THE BOX ROOM

It all starts with a free corrugated box. The flaps on one end are cut off and the back flaps are pushed out to make the box deeper. A new back from an extra box is attached with strong mailing tape. The finished dimensions are 18" wide, 12" high and 16" deep.

The layout includes a kitchenette, a balcony (this is a very high apartment) and fake storage drawers and closet between the two areas. The kitchen site area measures 6" wide and 7½" deep, and is one step up from the rest of the room.

An apple green, terry hand towel becomes the wall-to-wall carpeting and establishes the color scheme. The walls are finished off with left-over white pebble board and green and white patterned wallpaper. When a striped design paper is turned horizontal, it takes on a surprisingly modern appearance. The same striped paper covers the two "doors" and simulated drawers for design interest. Vinyl from a sample book is used for the kitchen floor and balcony floor. The great

Fig. 11–1 This one-room efficiency apartment was made almost completely from scrap. The color scheme is green and white, which effectively includes the white plastic materials used for some furnishings. An acrylic front will easily slide between two wood moldings.

Fig. 11—2 Left-over fabrics, papers, plastic bread wrappings, ribbon holders, cork, film reels, egg shells, Cracker-Jack pop sticks, vegetable seeds, paper cups, room deodorant packaging, foam packaging, formica scraps, cheese wax covering, glass bottles and salad bowls gain a second life in reuse.

Fig. 11—3 The shell of the corrugated box is further strengthened with white pebble matboard walls and cardboard covered with wallpaper. The main portion of the floor is an apple green, terry cloth hand towel. Kitchen floor and balcony floor are vinyls from a sample book. The make-believe doors and drawers are covered with matching wallpaper for a decorative touch. The door on left side leads to a bathroom-dressing room area.

Fig. 11–4 The balcony terrace overlooks a mountain scene cut from a magazine. The railing is cut from hardware cloth and painted black. Plastic furnishings, a wall lamp, seashell planter and a rock in the corner fill out the bare spaces. Terrace is finished off before inside wall is put in place.

mountain view from the balcony is a magazine cut-out, and the balcony railing is cut from hardware cloth (¼″ mesh), painted black.

The simulated sliding door is a ¹/₁₆″ acrylic cut to fit opening. The edges and center vertical piece are strips of aluminum cut from a frozen-dinner plate. Single strip is glued down center section, and the entire piece is pressed into opening after balcony furnishings are completed.

Kitchen cabinets and appliances are designed and planned on paper for fit. Finished wall cabinets are stained basswood and are glued onto wall. Refrigerator is made out of olive green mat board, as is front of stove. Front of sink is stained basswood, matching cabinets. A fluorette bulb is attached to underside of cabinets. The bulb is powered by a 3-volt battery holder by Illinois Hobbycraft.

Fig. 11–5 The kitchenette cabinets are made from basswood (stained), and olive green matboard is used for the appliances. The sink is a jelly container from a restaurant, with a doo-dad faucet. The burners on the electric stovetop are formed heavy aluminum, topped with black-painted, coiled florist's wire. The three bowls are made from eggshells.

White plastic ribbon winders with a diagonal design are cut and placed in two different positions to become room dividers. The door on the left leads into an imaginary bath-dressing room area and the shower cap on the door knob is made from plastic bread wrapping.

The outside of the corrugated box can be covered with wallpaper, vinyl, colored board or anything available.

Fig. 11–6 A view of the completed kitchenette. A fluorette bulb attached to the cabinet over sink is electrified. Used film spools become table legs and stools. The white plastic divider is a portion of a ribbon winder.

## SOFA BED

### *Materials*

$^1\!/_2''$ balsa wood; $^5\!/_8''$ dowel; art foam; $^1\!/_2''$ polyurethane or sponge; upholstery fabric; illustration board: Velverette glue.

### *Directions*

1. Groove out top B to allow dowel C to fit.
2. Glue each dowel into place atop B. Sand ends for smoothness.
3. Cut illustration board D 3" × 6". Glue board on top of two pieces of A.
4. Glue art foam up, over and down pieces B and C. Cover pieces A and D with art foam.
5. Cut cushion from $^1\!/_2''$ polyurethane. Cover with fabric, and add "piping" if desired.

### Upholstery

1. Cut fabric for front and back of both arms. Allow an extra $^1\!/_8''$ for fold-over. Two pieces will be reversed. Clip in $^1\!/_8''$ on curved area. See drawing #1 on Fig. 11–7.
2. Glue fabric to the four arm ends. Press down well. When dry, clip away excess bulges of fabric with scissors.
3. Cut two pieces of fabric 3" wide to fit up, over and down each armpiece. Start applying glue along outside edges of arm and along crease of roll. Glue fabric in place, pressing into curve area with nails. Continue gluing rest of edges and press fabric down. Cut away excess at bottom.
4. Cut fabric to wrap around base piece A and D. Add extra $^1\!/_2''$ allowance. Glue in place underneath structure and along sides. Clip away excess at corners as you glue.
5. Add "piping" (crochet thread or embroidery floss) along joined edges on arm pieces. Piping can be matching or contrasting color.
6. Glue three sections together. Top with fabric-covered (polyurethane) cushion.

## SHOW-TOP TABLE

Loose powder boxes made of plastic resemble a drum table. The bottom part turned upside down provides a nice recessed niche for showing off collectible items, in this case miniature seashells. A round of sandpaper is cut to fit and is glued into place. Tiny seashells are glued onto the sandpaper. A round of acetate (from stationery box) is cut to fit outermost edges of top. Evenly spaced sequin pins are glued through acetate and into drilled holes on box top to secure acetate top. This box is white but they also come in other colors.

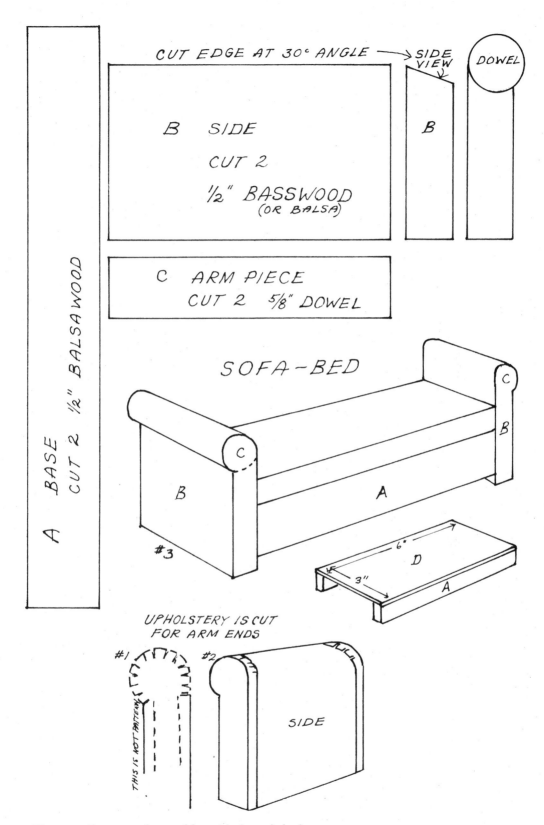

CUT EDGE AT 30° ANGLE → SIDE VIEW

DOWEL

B SIDE

CUT 2

½" BASSWOOD
(OR BALSA)

B

C ARM PIECE
CUT 2   ⅝" DOWEL

A BASE
CUT 2 ½" BALSAWOOD

SOFA-BED

C

B

B

A

#3

D

6"

3"

A

UPHOLSTERY IS CUT
FOR ARM ENDS

#1   #2

THIS IS NOT PATTERN

SIDE

Fig. 11–7 Pattern and assembly guide for sofa-bed.

## BENCH

If you don't have an extra wooden salad bowl, you can purchase an inexpensive one at the variety store. Mark 1¼" of space through the *center* of the bowl. Saw the two end pieces away with a power tool. Cut a ⅛" thick piece of wood to fit across for the seat A. Finish to match the rest of the bench, and glue into place. Cut ¼" foam cushion to fit seat and cover with material. Make three pillows for back of bench if desired.

## BEAN BAG CHAIR

### *Materials*

Soft supple leather or marshmallow plastic material; ⅓ cup raw rice.

### *Directions*

1. Place two pieces A together, *right sides together*. Stitch or sew along one side approximately ⅛" in from edge.

2. Continue sewing on each piece until all six pieces of A are sewn together.

3. Material still wrong side out, lay circle piece B onto one end, right side facing inward. Sew circle to ends of A. Use a locking stitch when sewing to secure a good closing.

4. Carefully clip curved edges of pieces.

5. Turn material right side out.

6. Pour rice into bag.

7. Using overlapping stitch, sew second circle piece to folded-in ends of A to close bag.

8. Punch the bag into chair shape.

Fig. 11–8 Sections of sofa-bed are covered with art foam before being glued together.

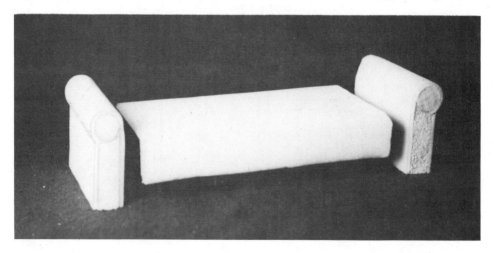

Fig. 11–9 The white plastic drum table is an upended bottom section from a loose powder box. Round top is held in place with four sequin pins. Table lamp is unused sample bottle stuffed with seashells. Rock formation is mounted as an interesting art object. The sofa-bed is covered with soft green velvet, and trimmed with green crochet thread. On the floor a rock resembled a monkey figure; some inked features were added and the "monkey" was placed on a piece of driftwood. The stand holding the modeled head is a film reel; the center is covered with mottled contact paper. The bean bag chair used left-over marshmallow plastic fabric; the clogs are carved out of pine. The lamp is 18-gauge wire, a button shank and wooden base. The framed pigeons were cut from a direct mail advertisement.

## ACCESSORIES FROM SCRAP

### "Love" Clock

Use sharp knife and needle files to round edges and shape the letters. Wood may be stained or painted, as desired. Cover letter O with cutout of a clock face, or use watch parts. Add hands of clock.

### Television Set

Basic box starts with a square bottle top. This one is from a Maybelline Moisture Make-Up bottle. Black card is cut and fitted to fill open area. Rectangular opening is cut out of black card. A white line is painted around the opening, and clear acetate and gray paper are glued over opening for TV screen. Entire front panel is fastened into front of plastic box. Knobs are made from pin heads, links and gold beads.

### Tea Kettle

There are all kinds of tea kettles, but some contemporary ones seem to have lost part of their handle. This one starts with a white rubber bumper with the spike removed. A cover (tack top and bead) is glued on top. Plastic ballpoint pen tubing is added for spout, and a cut earring part becomes the handle. This kettle was painted olive green with white flowers; the top and handle are black.

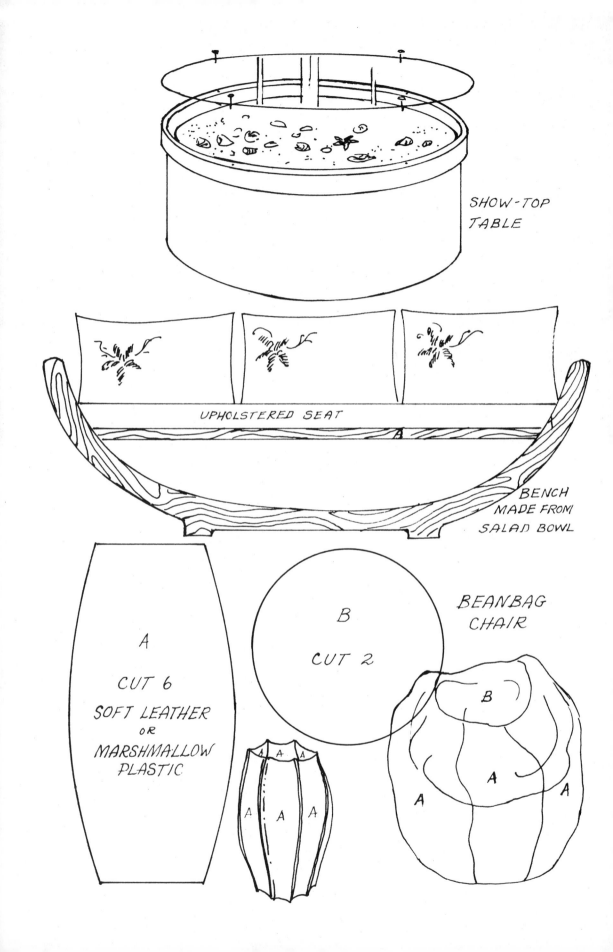

SHOW-TOP
TABLE

UPHOLSTERED SEAT

BENCH
MADE FROM
SALAD BOWL

BEANBAG
CHAIR

A

CUT 6

SOFT LEATHER
OR
MARSHMALLOW
PLASTIC

B

CUT 2

Fig. 11—11 The bench seat made from a sliced section of a wooden salad bowl is upholstered in white marshmallow plastic. The wall screen is from room deodorant packaging. The television set starts with a square Mabelline cosmetic bottle top, and a tooled leather bucket is the end of a leather belt. Love clock is carved wood with scrap watch parts.

## Rock Sculpture

A small round cork and black-painted toothpick form the base for a polished rock (see Fig. 11—9).

## Wooden Clogs

Cut two pieces of hardwood $5/8'' \times 5/16'' \times 1/4''$. Following the suggested cut-away lines as shown in Fig. 11—12, carefully carve away portions of wood until clog shape is acquired. Glue leather top into place.

## Bowls

Bowls are made from the rounded end of discarded eggshells. Use very sharp cuticle scissors; not all cuttings will be perfect. I got three good cuttings from twelve eggs. Wash shell and carefully remove

Fig. 11—10 Pattern and assembly guide for show-top table, bench with upholstered seat, and a bean bag chair.

CLOCK

TELEVISION

ROCK SCULPTURE

CLOGS

TEA KETTLE

BOWLS

SHOWER CAP

CANDLES

KNOTHOLE ART

DRIED ARRANGEMENT

FLOOR LAMP

PUSSY WILLOWS

inside membrane. Cover outer surface of shell with diluted white glue, and dry upside down. Then cover inner surface of shell with same glue. Glue strengthens the shell. Rim of bowl may need sanding for a smooth finish. I used BO-READO acrylic tube paints for these bowls. When design is dry, cover with one application of a "glass finish" or use an acrylic spray for a glazed effect.

### Dried Flower Arrangement

An impressive dried flower arrangement can be made from dried seeds. Salvage these throw-away items from apples and green peppers and quickly dig out some small cucumber seeds when no one is looking. Set them aside to dry. When ready, glue into petal shapes on the tips of any *thin* dried grass stalks. Use tiny bits of cotton to help hold seeds. Apple seeds are best, split in two. Add lots of extra stalks for added fullness and interest. I used a purchased (owl) macrame bead as a container.

### Shower Cap

Bread plastic wrappings have some very interesting designs, and can become a lovely shower cap. A very fine, sharp needle is used to gather stitches along the edge. Gently and firmly pulled in, a shower cap takes shape. These wrappings also make nice shower curtains.

### Candles

The outside wax covering of Edam, Bonbel, Gouda and other cheeses becomes a most responsive modeling compound between warm fingers. The wax colors vary from cheese to cheese and with a little manipulation you can produce some contemporary candles.

Two colors of wax (rose and yellow) can be worked together to form another color, peach. Interesting variations can be achieved by winding a thin strip of one color wax (red) around a different color wax (yellow) and rolling them both gently on a flat surface. Three colors can be stacked atop each other, rolled and a three color fat candle will be formed.

### Floor Lamp

The lamp consists of three pieces: a button shank, 18-gauge wire and a block of wood. Top of wire is soldered to button shank. Wire is shaped, and the end is glued into drilled hole in wooden block (stained or painted). A small decorative metal piece can be glued on the block for extra support.

### Knothole Art

The pussy cat painting on basswood (or any wood) starts with a small knothole, which becomes the eye of the painted subject. The cat

Fig. 11–12 Assembly for various room accessories.

Fig. 11–13 These dried "flowers" are made from dried grass stalks and seeds from apples, cucumbers and green peppers. The macrame owl bead is a perfect holder.

is orange with brown striping and features. A tiny black mouse keeps the kitty company. After painting, the surface is coated with several applications of diluted white glue for a smooth satiny finish.

### Pussy Willows

Select some very thin stalks with branches. I used the tops of Chinese Pennies. If color of stalks is light, paint brown or rust. Roll the *tiniest* of oval cotton balls; a little saliva helps. Let balls dry and then glue onto branches, turning all around. Dry. With acrylic paint and small brush, color the balls with combinations of gray and ochre.

# PART III

# ROOMS
# by GUEST
# MINIATURISTS

# 12

# A Gallery of Rooms and Shops

WHEN I approached several people about contributing their work for my new book of miniatures, I expressly mentioned that "contemporary" would be the theme. It was no great surprise to me to learn that everyone's idea of "contemporary" was indeed varied. Suffice to say that all contributions and interpretations were warmly welcomed and appreciated.

## BURNED BAMBOO PLANT STAND

by DEE SNYDER

See Figs. 12–5 and 12–6.

### *Materials*

Six swab sticks cut to 3¾" long, scored with file or X-ACTO blade to resemble bamboo; ⅛" balsa for top and bottom shelf; scraps of small half-round or toothpicks to add a trim to top and shelf and ¾" down from top; stain or paint to finish.

### *Directions*

1. Cut out top and shelf from balsa. Make holes on underside of top.
2. Score six legs to resemble bamboo.
3. Glue legs to top and shelf in place; work upside down.
4. When dry, add "bamboo" trim to edges of top, shelf and as support ¾" down from top.
5. Stain or finish as desired.

(Above) Fig. 12–1 This beautiful contemporary Living Room, Dining Room and Study above Kitchen was designed and built by master craftsman, Peter Westcott. The box is 30″ wide by 24″ deep by 18″ high. Off the kitchen there is a patio which adds an extra dimension of depth and space to the already expansive rooms. The basic box is made from ½″ plywood with all the interior construction made from basswood. The fireplace and barbecue fireplace (patio) are made from Cell-u-clay and painted with latex paint. The floor and ceiling are pine boards stained and finished with urethane. Using a high and low post construction for the columns and then running the ceiling boards to each beam, a double curve is produced. The interior furniture, designed and constructed by Peter, is made from stained basswood. The dining table and coffee table are solid walnut with a urethane finish. The legs of the dining table are mirrored formica. The chairs are ⅛″ acrylic. The plastic sculpture at right is called "Family." (Neil Koppes, photograph)

(Right) Fig. 12–2 The patio is 30″ wide, 10″ deep and 18″ high and is obviously meant for pleasure. The patio is well laid out, with a stepup area to a rock garden display. The plantings of bushes and trees made from lychen contrast with the wooden fence and stonework of the patio floor and walls. No patio is complete without a barbecue pit and eating facilities, and Peter Westcott includes both in this original layout. (Neil Koppes, photograph)

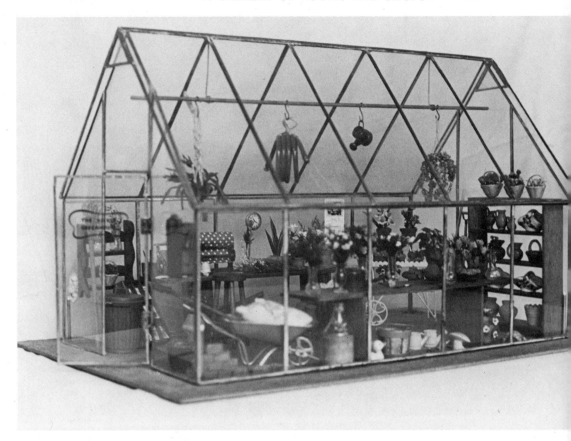

Fig. 12–4 The Silver Greenhouse is a combined effort by Jeanette and Martha Silver. Both took a course in stained glass-making and used those techniques to construct the greenhouse from regular plate glass. They made the shelves, counters and seed rack from balsa wood. They folded little pieces of white paper into seed packets, labeled them and drew pictures to represent different flowers and vegetables. They also quilled some flowers and the rest are purchased bread dough creations. (Fred Mushel, photograph)

Fig. 12–3 Norman Forgue has an extensive collection of miniature rooms, all self-made. Among the group is this formal Dining Room. The furnishings were made by Norman, and many accessories are contrived. Look closely at the set table. Cups, saucers and teapot were turned on lathe from pine, lacquered, then sprayed with Zimms super glaze. (Larry De Vera, photograph)

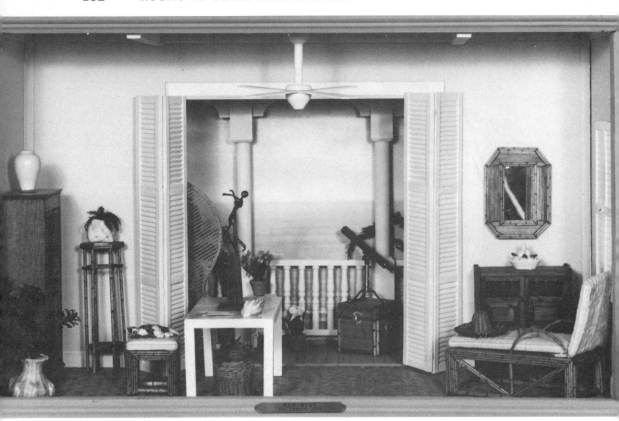

Fig. 12–5 Key West is visited by many vacationers. Intrigued and inspired by variations of architecture and tropical flavor, Dee Snyder created a dream retreat by the sea with this Key West room. In a shadow box room, 18″ × 11″ × 12″, pale mauve walls, white ceiling, white woodwork and yellow accessories complement each other. The room floor is covered with an old lahala placemat. The balcony in front of a papered seascape scene is constructed from available parts. Dee made most of the furnishings, including the white Parsons table, bamboo chaise, tall bamboo plant stand, Chinese wicker chest, peacock wicker chair (on balcony), bamboo mirror and bench. Her own handmade accessories include the ceramic lemons in a basket, a jar, palm fan, paddle ceiling fan and Hemingway book. The metal sculpture of a man (center) is by a Florida artist, Chet Spatcher. (Merrill Green, photograph)

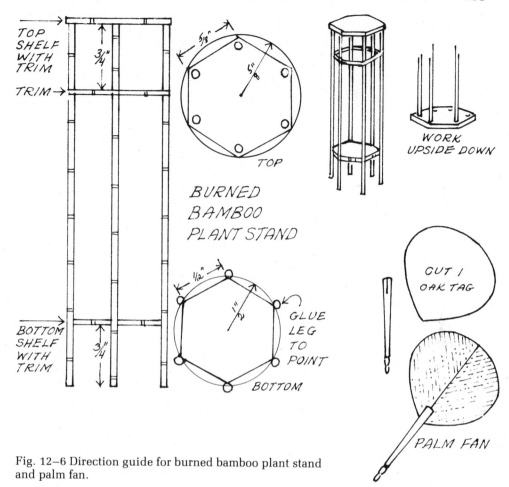

Fig. 12–6 Direction guide for burned bamboo plant stand and palm fan.

## PALM FAN

by DEE SNYDER

### *Materials*

Oak tag; round toothpick; scrap of grass cloth, lahola mat or straw place mat.

### *Directions*

1. Cover oak tag cut-out with any of the above mentioned scraps. Grass cloth would be applied diagonally as shown in Fig. 12–6.

2. Cut toothpick in half. Shape handle and file turnings at tip. Split top to fit on fan. Glue in place.

3. Add a little stain to handle.

Fig. 12–7 When Kitty McKenna decided to have a Dollhouse Shop and husband John agreed to make it, she put some extra thought into it. Kitty designed the front of the "building" and John put it together. The size of the front is 19¹/₂″ wide by 16¹/₂″ high. The door and window are ready-made but the latter was modified to fit space and design. A few days' effort went into steaming and weighting boards to acquire the curve of the roof. Shingles are made to 1″ scale from real house cedar shingles.

## ETAGERE

by MARILYN DAVIDSON and ELAINE FLEISCHMAN (Minis by M.E.)
See Figs. 12–12 and 12–13.

### *Materials*

Two rods or tubes at least 15″ long and ¹/₈″ outside diameter; clear acrylic ¹/₈″ thick for shelves, four pieces cut to 3″ × 1¹/₄″, or size desired; four beads doughnut shape or round, in colors to match rods. Suitable for rods—aluminum rods, brass tubing or chrome if available. Brass tube may be plated for a chrome finish after bending.

Fig. 12–8 Inside the Dollhouse Shop by Kitty and John McKenna, Mr. Peepers, the proprietor, is showing off his biggest miniature domain, a castle. A small boy kneels on the floor examining a handmade house, one of three in the room. Other small houses include some old 1935 cardboard Christmas Tree decorations, a couple of antique tin buildings, and a few new tree decorations. On the floor is a hand-crocheted rug and on the right wall is a small house-shaped sign that reads, "We Carry Mini Mortgage Loans." The inside box dimensions are 19″ wide by 11″ high by 11″ deep.

### Directions

1. Use a can or similar round object around which tubes or rods can be bent without crimping. Diameter of object used will determine the width of etagere legs. Example: for a 3″ wide etagere a tuna fish can is the right size. Mark the mid point of rod and, holding that point against a smooth portion of the can, bend rod so that the bend is equidistant from marked point. See Fig. 12–13. When both rods are bent to the same shape, stand them up together to be sure that the legs are equidistant and that the tops are equally curved and legs are

Fig. 12–9 When someone loves art you give them an art gallery. That's why Jeanette and Martha Silver gave Evelyn's Art Gallery to their mother. They made over half the picture frames from miniature molding. Some of the pictures are classics printed on silk, and others are from magazines or greeting cards. The door was made from basswood, and the "stained glass" was a piece of purchased acetate. The lower floor and upper level was parqueted with commercial wood veneer. The handrail for the stairs and the guardrail on the second floor were constructed from brass tubing bought in a hobby shop. The dimensions for this room are 21″ wide by 9″ deep by 17″ high. (Fred Mushel, photograph)

Fig. 12–10 Just when you think you've seen them all, along come Jane and Will Hagenbuch who construct miniature aquariums. The Wharf, 20″ wide, 18″ high and 12″ deep, is a perfect example of their specialty. This rendition was made from weathered board from a back fence, and the aquarium (holding one gallon of water) is 3″ deep by 14″ wide by 8″ high. The working aquarium contains an air filter, gravel and greenery just like its big counterpart. Two guppies and one sucker fish are very much "at home" in a natural environment. Sylvia Olson is the lucky owner of The Wharf. (Will Hagenbuch, photograph)

slightly splayed. At this point, rods should be chrome plated, if desired. If brass is used, polish and finish to prevent tarnishing.

2. For shelves (using acrylic, cut to size desired), edges must be sanded, polished and buffed until they are crystal clear and sparkle. Usually a buffing wheel, buffing discs and polishing compound are needed to finish the plastic properly. Follow directions for finishing acrylics (available at most libraries). Drill holes in corners of each shelf, making sure that all holes line up exactly; diameter of hole should be the same as finished diameter of tube or rod.

3. Insert all legs of etagere into holes provided and adjust height of each shelf.

4. Place one bead at bottom of each leg and glue into place. Lower bottom shelf to steady etagere. It is preferable to get a little glue to join the bottom shelf to the beads so that the finished product will stand sturdily. The slightly splayed legs will put pressure on the shelves and keep them in place.

Fig. 12–11 The Library by Norman Forgue gathers together all the clutter created by the man of the family. Norman made all furnishings except the rocker and doll figures. The fireplace is an HO tunnel portal; it has a light coat of red wash, and the seams are filled with white paint, trimmed in gray. Books are printer's quads covered with leather, cloth and decorative papers. The rug is made from cotton print, edged with black braid. (Larry De Vera, photograph)

Fig. 12–12 This contemporary dining room was made by Marilyn Davidson and Elaine Fleischman (Minis by M.E.). Using the see-through airy touch of Lucite for principal furnishings, their dining room is most modern and sophisticated. The floor is softly carpeted, and the patterned wall covering makes an interesting background for transparent furniture. Everything in the room is an original design. (Photo Illustration Center, photograph)

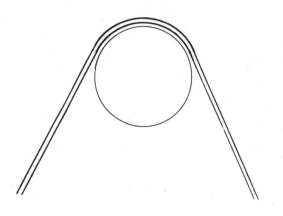

*1. BEND RODS AROUND SMOOTH ROUND OBJECT*

### ETAGERE

*2. CUT 4 1/8" ACRYLIC*

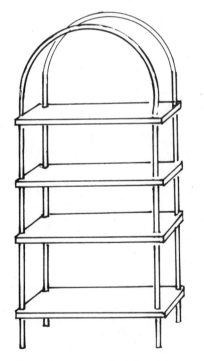

*3. ADJUST SHELVES TO DESIRED SPACING*

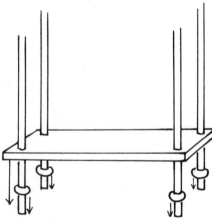

*4. SLIDE SHELF AND BEAD DOWN UNTIL BEAD RESTS ON WORK SURFACE. GLUE WILL SEEP UP AND SLIGHTLY TOUCH SHELF.*

Fig. 12−13 Direction guide for etagere.

Fig. 12–14 Antique Shops will always be popular, and Jeanette and Martha Silver made this miniature rendition. The dimensions of the room are 18" wide by 10" deep by 11" high. The box was a commercial kit that they glued, painted and stained. They built shelves for the left and right sides to display more objects. (Fred Mushel, photograph)

Fig. 12–15 Mildred Herbig expresses her own hidden desires, creating a charming pink, white and green "dream bedroom" for little girls. The window (Houseworks) was reversed in order to build bookcases around it. Most items in the room were designed and made by Mildred. The fireplace is an X-ACTO kit; bed, blanket chest and night stand are from Diminutiques by Jean Dickey; and the rocker is a Mel Prescott pattern with an added crochet edging. French knots worked loosely on the bed and window furnishings incorporate an idea suggested by Linda Long to create a ball-fringe illusion. (Robert Kelley, photograph)

Fig. 12—16 Over the years Kitty McKenna gathered many interesting items for a western Tack Shop. Some are inexpensive, such as buckets and Mexican shoes and boots. Others include quality creations of embossed cowboy boots, horse collar mirror (front), embossed bridle, horse blanket (left wall) and some hats by Sylvia Rountree. Kitty has added her own creative bit with handmade bridles and halters from scrap coat leather, some shoulder handbags, saddle blankets on the shelf, a cobbler's bench, and saw horse. This shop is one of many in a little village that Kitty and John McKenna have created. The front has been removed, which accounts for the foliage in foreground.

## TREE HOUSE

by KITTY MCKENNA

See Figs. 12—18 and 12—19.

Acquire a limb about three to four feet long at the start. The diameter of main branch (trunk) should be about ³/₄″. The main section is cut about 14″ up, leaving some branches below cut. Mark for center front.

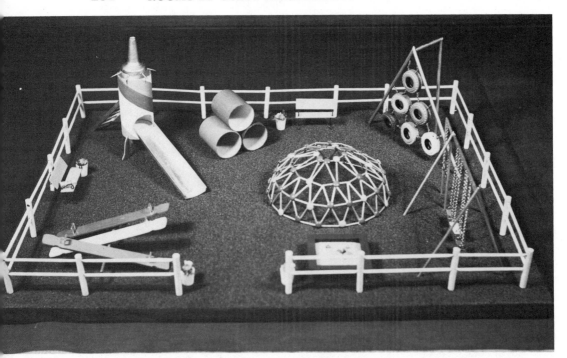

Fig. 12–17 When you have two boys, a children's playground is a "natural" subject to make, and Marion Cole did just that. Vivid in color and thoughtfully planned, each play unit is carefully constructed from a selection of wood strips and sheets, dowels, cardboard tubing, chain, toothpicks, thumb tacks, wire, toothpaste tube caps and a couple of "borrowed" items from model hobby sets. One climbing gym, upper right, is made from hobby toy tires, chain and dowel sticks. The see-saws even have three grooved areas underneath each board to accommodate the difference in weight distribution of its users.

Dissect piece by piece. Carefully remove the twigs as you go along, leaving the ones on the bottom as is *below* the main cut. Lay the others on the floor as they are severed *in the order cut.* Later they will be reattached.

### Foundation

Cut a ³/₄″ thick round of wood with 11¹/₂″ diameter; drill a hole in center to fit the size of lower main branch. Glue the bottom of the branch and insert in hole. When dry, drill a small hole up in the branch bottom and into "trunk" bottom. Hammer nail through both for extra steadiness.

### Floor

Lay two beams across through the branches where fit is best. Anchor them. Lay the floor around main "trunk" of tree and leave a

Fig. 12—18 Gulliverville, the town that Kitty and John McKenna created, had just about everything except a tree house, so the "Rinky Dink Club House" came into being. When the "right branch" was finally approved, construction started. Limbs were cut away; some were discarded and others were glued back later. The structure includes all the extras such as a kite snarled in the branches, a pulley and rope with a basket for "goodies," a tire swing and, of course, a ladder from scraps attached to the trunk. Flowers and leaves were added from the remains of an old Easter hat.

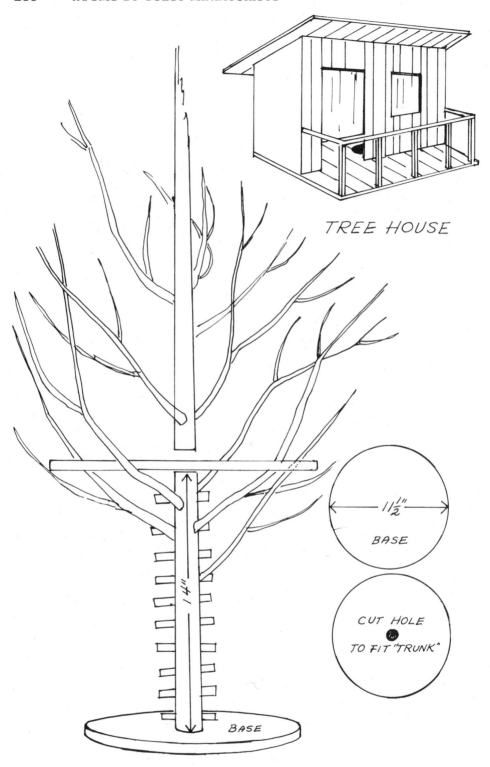

TREE HOUSE

BASE

CUT HOLE
TO FIT "TRUNK"

BASE

Fig. 12–19 Construction guide to the Tree House.

Fig. 12–20 Striking black and gold contact paper sets off the walls of this spacious Bathroom. Norman Forgue put all the necessities and more into his miniature room. All furnishings were made from scratch; fixtures are actual porcelain made in rubber molds, then glazed and fired with dubonnet color added. The shower curtain is made from ½" strips of ribbon joined with glue, and the back wall is tile. The odds and ends are made from jewelry findings. Notice the hand protruding from the curtain dropping the last bit of clothing. (Larry De Vera, photograph)

Fig. 12–21 Cheese boxes don't have to end up as trash. Eunice and Dick Tabor innovatively created a series of twelve monthly scenes using round cheese boxes for vignettes. A reprint of the Smokey Mountains is a good background for this Camping Scene. The plywood floor is covered with grasslike matting. The Tabors designed and made the tent and duffle bags using material from a discarded quilted nylon winter ski jacket. The sleeping bags are bright blue quilted material from bedspreads. The picnic table is a purchase as is the grill which is "old." Other little accessories were acquired from miniature shops. (Steve Woiler, photograph)

hole near trunk for entrance to house. This floor is 10″ by 12″ with 1½″ of this reserved for the porch. The house height is 6¾″ at front, sloping to 5¾″ at rear. Smaller floor dimensions can be used if preferred.

Continue building the framework of house, leaving openings for door and window to porch.

Carefully reattach twigs. The *center* trunk is put back in place, reinforced by drilling and inserting dowels through connecting ends.

Fig. 12–22 The owner of The Sports Shop has updated his exterior facade with a modernized window. The shop was designed and built by John McKenna and trimmed and stocked by Kitty McKenna. The window display is tastefully done with a nice selection of sports equipment acquired at various times. The basketball player is a cake decoration; the football is a coat button; the canoe is a celuloid novelty from an antique shop.

## House

After tree has been put back together, finish exterior of house with weathered board or whatever. Add roof around the main tree trunk. You may want to add some crude furniture before roofing. Add rails to porch. Add more branches if needed or trim tips if needed.

Make a ladder; add scraps of wood to tree trunk from bottom to floor entrance.

Fig. 12–23 Constructed by John McKenna, the interior of The Sports Shop carries through with Northeastern brick pattern on the back wall—the same that is used on the front facade. Display shelves hold purchased and handmade sports equipment. Ski patches are added wall decorations. Kitty McKenna made the winter hats and scarves, snowmobile mittens, ammo boxes and skis (from popsicle sticks). The two dolls were made by Mrs. Schink.

### Base

Cover the bottom with some green grass paper or whatever will simulate grass or camouflage with bushes, rocks or other "earthy" products, perhaps flowers except where the ladder starts.

### Extras

Add a basket with a pulley attachment; snarl a kite within the branches; set a fresh baked pie upon the porch; add some spring blossoms and leaves to the branches. And don't forget a little boy doll and his poochie to enjoy it.

Fig. 12–24 Anyone would love to sit upon a stool and be served an ice cream delicacy in this Soda Fountain vignette. Jeanette and Martha Silver constructed the box from 1/4″ luan wood. It measures 10″ wide by 4″ deep by 8½″ high. A piece of acetate covers the front to protect the objects from dust. (Fred Mushel, photograph)

*Finally,*
*    "hats off"*
*        to all miniaturists,*
*            everywhere*

Derby hat miniature squirrel house
created by Kitty McKenna

# ...es of Supply

...E knows what SOS means. In this case, it appropriately ... with Sources of Supply.

... number of sources are listed for the benefit of any new ...ho need help in getting started. There are a vast number ...l sources waiting to offer service. These can be found ...vertisements in magazines, bulletins, newsletters, ...d at miniature shows. Always include a large, self-...ped envelope (SASE) when inquiring.

## ...S

...land; Alice Robbins, P.O. Box 62, Ramsey, NJ 07446. ...cessories of excellent quality; mini dolls, animals, toys ...more. Brochure 50¢, plus long SASE.

...Things; The Fieldwood Company, P.O. Box 223B, ..., NJ 07423. A large assortment of things for the ...; also lists building, electrical, masonry supplies and ...log $2.00)

... also included in catalogs from The Dollhouse Factory ... Miniatures (see Construction section).

## ...INGS AND NOTIONS

...tlet, Donna Murray, (moved to) 37A–RD 1, Lisbon, NY ... buttons, fabrics, trims, laces, ribbons, miniatures and ... (No catalog).

JAF Miniatures, 8400 East 105th Street, Kansas City, MO 64134. Also brass findings; tubing; Austrian cut crystal and Czech glass beads; miniatures and more. (Catalog #4, $2.50).

## BOOKS ON DOLLHOUSES, MINIATURES AND DOLLS

Paul A. Ruddell, Hobby House Press, 4701 Queensbury Road, Riverdale, MD 20840. Extensive descriptive listing of books dealing with history, patterns and how-to-do. (Catalog free).

## CONSTRUCTION MATERIALS

Architectural Model Supplies, Inc., 115-B Bellam Boulevard, P.O. Box 3497, San Rafael, CA 94902. Wood and moldings (Northeastern); trims; kits for furniture, windows, doors; tools; hardware; wallpaper; paints; embossed materials; instruction books and more. (Catalog #4, $4.00).

Carlson's Miniatures, Rt. #1, Box 306, Delavan, WI 53115. Building components, doors, windows, etc.; staircases; miniature pine furniture and more. (Catalog $1.00). Wholesale requests must include resale tax number.

The Dollhouse Factory, Box 456, 157 Main Street, Lebanon, NJ 08833. Wood and moldings (Northeastern); hardware; band and power tools; ready-made components; accessories and furniture; kits; wallpaper; shadow boxes; dolls; instruction books and more. (Catalog $2.00)

Northeastern Scale Models, Inc., Box 425, Mathuen, MA 01844. Wood products for construction work. See your dealer first. (SASE for catalog or catalog and samples, $1.00)

Shaker Miniatures, 2913 Huntington Road, Cleveland, OH 44120. Wood and moldings (Northeastern); components for building including windows, doors, fireplaces; hinges; tools; electric components and more. (Catalog $1.50).

## DISPLAY BOXES OR ROOMS

Big Ben, P.O. Box 207, Ridgewood, NJ 07451. Shadow boxes, vignettes and other specialty items. (Brochure $1.00).

Peter F. Westcott, 910 N. 24th Street, Phoenix, AZ 85008. Custom-designed box rooms and limited edition furniture. (SASE for inquiry).

Also The Dollhouse Factory (see Construction materials above). Kits for rooms, shadow boxes and vignettes.

## ELECTRICAL APPLIANCES

Cir-Kit Concepts, Inc., 608 North Broadway, Rochester, MN 55901. A "tape-on" wiring system. (Catalog $2.00).

Elegant Electric, division of Enchanted Toy Shop, 23812 Lorain Road, North Olmstead, OH 44070. Fixtures and component parts. (Catalog 75¢, refundable with first order).

Electrical Appliances are also listed within other catalogues: The
Dollhouse Factory; Shaker Miniatures; Architectural Model
Supplies.

## GUIDE BOOK OF SOURCES

Guide to American Miniaturists, Fourth Edition; Jane Haskell, 31
Evergreen Road, Northford, CT 06472. Lists descriptive sources
for miniatures by craftsmen, dealers and shops. Geographical and
alphabetical index. Other information included. Softbound book is
$4.25, plus $1.00 postage.

One Twelfth; One Twelfth Publishing Company, P.O. Box 107 R,
Norwalk, CT 06856. Lists hundreds of sources in geographical and
alphabetical order. Periodicals and museums listed. Other information included. Softbound book is $4.95, plus 75¢ postage.

The Miniatures Catalog, Third Edition; Boynton and Associates, Clifton House, Clifton, VA 22024. Illustrated, descriptive guide to
miniature houses, building components, furniture, accessories,
books, plans and tools. Softbound catalog is $12.00 plus $1.00 for
postage and handling.

## LAMPS

Bob Wittman, 647 Hewey Street, Utica, NY 13502. Lamps are ready to
be filled with your own scene. Also box rooms, dollhouses, stone
fireplaces. (No catalog; SASE for inquiry.)

## METAL SHAPES AND TUBING

K and S Engineering, 6917 West 59th Street, Chicago, IL 60638.
(Catalog is 25¢).

Also some shapes are offered in catalog of JAF Miniatures. (see above).

## NEEDLEWORK KITS

Create Your Own, Catherine Callas Knowles, Hickory Corner Rd., R.R.
#2, Milford, NJ 08848. Needlepoint (petit point) kits for rugs,
chairs, stools, bell pulls; crewel and embroidery kits for quilts,
draperies, linens, etc. (Catalog—send long SASE, two stamps).

Miniatures in Needlework, Meg Nyberg, 133 Onondaga Street, Corn-
ing, NY 14830. Latch-hook rug designs and kits, punch needles.
Description and price list sheet, free with SASE. Color prints of
various rugs are 50¢ a piece, refundable with first order.

Doreen Sinnett Designs, 418 Santa Ana Avenue, P.O. Box 2055, New-
port Beach, CA 92663. Mini-hooker dollhouse rug kits, patterns,
punch needles. Also dolls, papier-mâché bricks and shingles.
(Information—large SASE; complete catalog $2.00)

## TOOLS

Brookstone Company, 120 Vose Farm Road, Peterborough, NH 03458. Interesting, different and fine-quality tools. (Catalog $1.00, subsequent catalogs will follow).

Dremel Manufacturing Division, 4195 21st Street, Racine, WI 53406. Power tools (use local dealer).

X-ACTO, 4535 Van Dam Street, Long Island City, NY 11101. Basic tools, both manual and power. (Use local dealer). X-ACTO also furnishes shadow box room kits, rug kits, wallpapers, moldings and more.

Some tool suppliers are listed under **Construction materials.**

## WOOD (COMMERCIAL)

Albert Constantine and Sons, 2050 Eastchester Road, Bronx, NY 10461. (catalog 50¢).

Craftsman Wood Service Co., 1735 West Cortland Ct., Addison, IL 60101 (catalog 46 50¢).

# Newsletters and Publications

The *Doll House and Miniature News*, 3 Orchard Lane, Kirkwood, MO 63122. Published monthly except July and August (10 issues) $12.50; $13.50 for 1st class.

*International Dolls' House News*, 56 Lincoln Wood, Haywards Heath, Sussex, RH 16 1LH, England. Published quarterly; $10.75 check.

*Miniature Collector*, 170 Fifth Avenue, New York, NY 10010. Published bi-monthly; $9.97 US, $11.00 Canada, $12.00 foreign.

*Miniature Gazette* (publication of National Association of Miniature Enthusiasts), N.A.M.E., P.O. Box 2621 Brookhurst Center, Anaheim, CA 92804. Published quarterly. Send SASE for membership information, which includes *Gazette*.

*Nutshell News*, Clifton House, Clifton, VA 22024. Published monthly. $22.00 US, $24.00 Canada, $48.00 overseas airmail. Random sample copy $2.50 each.

The *Scale Cabinetmaker: A Journal for the Miniaturist*, Dorsett Miniatures, P.O. Box 87, Pembroke, VA 24136. Entirely how-to-build miniatures, etc. Published quarterly. $15.00 U.S. Sample issue $4.25 each.

*Small Talk*, Ark Graphics, P.O. Box 838, Capitola, Ca 95010. Published monthly. 12 issues for $12.00 US; Canada, Mexico and International rate $15.00; Single back issue $1.25.

# Index